Grace and Salvation

Grace and Salvation

Divine Engagement in Creation History

Dick O. Eugenio

RESOURCE *Publications* · Eugene, Oregon

GRACE AND SALVATION
Divine Engagement in Creation History

Copyright © 2022 Dick O. Eugenio. All rights reserved. Except for brief quotations in critical publications or reviews, no part of this book may be reproduced in any manner without prior written permission from the publisher. Write: Permissions, Wipf and Stock Publishers, 199 W. 8th Ave., Suite 3, Eugene, OR 97401.

Resource Publications
An Imprint of Wipf and Stock Publishers
199 W. 8th Ave., Suite 3
Eugene, OR 97401

www.wipfandstock.com

PAPERBACK ISBN: 978-1-6667-3720-2
HARDCOVER ISBN: 978-1-6667-9641-4
EBOOK ISBN: 978-1-6667-9642-1

04/01/22

All biblical quotations, unless otherwise indicated, are from the Holy Bible, New International Version®, NIV® Copyright ©1973, 1978, 1984, 2011 by Biblical, Inc.® Used by permission. All rights reserved worldwide.

To Jedidiah, beloved of God

Contents

Abbreviations | ix
Introduction | xi

1 Unmerited Beginnings | 1
2 Mystery of Iniquity | 11
3 One for the Many | 22
4 Relational Grace | 34
5 Restoration and Renewal | 50
6 Grace and Truth | 62
7 Embodied Saving Grace | 73
8 Salvific Gifts | 88
9 Empowering Grace | 101
10 Cosmic Salvation | 116

Bibliography | 129

Abbreviations

ANF	*Ante-Nicene Fathers*
Letters	*The Letters of John Wesley* (Telford edition)
NPNF2	*Nicene and Post-Nicene Fathers* (Second series)
Works (BE)	*Works of John Wesley* (Bicentennial edition)
Works (JE)	*The Works of Rev. John Wesley* (Jackson edition)

Introduction

GRACE AND SALVATION ARE two big terms. In fact, they are probably the most important topics of Christian conversations, and all other doctrinal affirmations are sometimes reduced to serve supporting roles. A quick Google search reveals that there is no scarcity of literature about each of them. Of course, they are ultimately inseparable. After all, salvation is by grace. How various Christian traditions understand this, however, marks the beginning of differences that have historically been the cause of bitter disagreement, resentment, and division within the one, holy, catholic church. Minute differences—because of nuanced interpretations and variegated emphases often grounded in unrecognized presuppositions and biases—result in schisms. This shows that understandings of grace and salvation are non-negotiable in all theological traditions.

Recent decades revealed an even deeper fascination of this tandem. Developments in biblical studies caused interest in re-constructing our long-held interpretations. The Reformation dictum "justification by grace through faith" is being evaluated in the light of a more holistic approach to the entire Bible. A call to return to the New Testament's Jewish roots guides theologians today to appropriate Hebrew thought and appreciate the continuity of salvation history from the time of creation. Insights about humanity created in the image of God, arguments about the vocation of humans as priests of creation, emphasis on the relationship between worship and mission, and zealous concerns for environmental care have also

Introduction

influenced the discussions about God's saving grace. All these themes are given attention here, although in varying degrees.

This book is unashamedly biblical and Wesleyan in its approach. First, it presents the biblical narrative from creation to the final consummation, highlighting elements of grace and salvation as progressively revealed in the Bible. Chapters 1–5 provide the Old Testament background. They offer a glimpse of how God operates as the gracious Savior. This is important because Jesus is born out of the womb of Israel, along with its history as the chosen people and its calling to bless the nations. In retrospect, we only understand the saving work of Jesus Christ through Israelite metaphors and symbols, its practices of worship and mission, its failure as a kingdom of priests, and its people's deep longing for salvation. When reading these chapters, we must keep in mind that salvific themes pervade Israelite history that point to Jesus Christ.

This book's presentation of grace and salvation begins from the very beginning of created time and space. The creation narrative reveals the generosity of God's nature, his design for well-being and harmony in the cosmos, and his inclusive invitation to "the different other" for loving communion. Unfortunately, creation's joy is interrupted by sin and its consequences. This is the theme of chapter 2. Sin and death replaced communion and life. But even in the darkest moment of salvation history, God's grace triumphs by giving hope and promising deliverance.

In chapter 3, we see God taking initiative in bringing humanity back to himself. He calls Abraham, whose offspring will become channels of blessing to the whole world. Through the one, many will be blessed. This theme emerges again in chapter 4, which deals with God's covenant with Israel. God delivers his beloved people from oppression and death. Various metaphors of salvation are also discussed, including what are entailed in God's deliverance. In particular, the missionary calling of the children of Abraham to be priests of creation is emphasized. God saves a nation and gives them a responsibility to the nations. Chapter 5 presents the consequences of Israel's failure to be God's holy people. Yet again, in the midst of the exile, themes and metaphors of saving grace emerge through the prophets. The Israelites are given hope and are promised renewal, not for their own sakes, but for them to fulfill their priestly vocation to the world.

Chapter 6 discusses the coming of the incarnate Son in the world. It highlights the fact that Israel disappoints Yahweh again. Jesus came to call Israel to repentance—to change their minds—concerning the shape,

Introduction

means, and scope of salvation. He preached a radical new way of kingdom life. If the Israelites were to become blessings to the nations, they have to see that the problem is sin and its solution is forgiveness, not violence. In addition, they have to see that the kingdom of God is for all. Chapter 7 explains how God indeed saves us from our sins and reconciles us to intimate relationship with him. It deals with what "the grace of the Lord Jesus Christ" is all about. His entire life—from his birth in Bethlehem to his presence at the right of the Father today—is redemptive. Major aspects of Jesus' redemptive life and work are presented, and in each, we see important elements of our salvation.

Chapters 8–10 underscore the spiritual blessings of saving grace. Chapter 8 deals with the gifts of salvation to humanity. We receive forgiveness of sins. We are reconciled with God. We become new creation. We are adopted as God's children. We are sanctified. These are the good news of the gospel. In addition, we receive the Holy Spirit, which is the theme of chapter 9. We must realize that salvation is the work of the Triune God. The Spirit works in prevenient grace to lead us to awakening and repentance. He opens our spiritual senses to see spiritual realities. He enables our human faculties to respond in obedience to God's call. The Spirit enkindles love in our hearts and empowers us to fulfill our God-given vocation in the world. In chapter 10, we see that God's saving grace is truly inclusive. The whole creation is the object of divine love. Christ died not only for humans, but to reconcile all things to God. We realize that humans are saved from sin and its effects, are renewed in his image, and are called back to intimacy with him, so that we can fulfill our mandate as stewards of creation. Through us as priests, the whole world will be blessed. The creation of the cosmos ends with the redemption of the cosmos. This is God's grace and salvation.

This book would not have been completed without the meticulous guidance from Al Truesdale and Alex Varughese. They have helped me greatly in rooting my arguments in biblical foundations and leading me to various contemporary resources. This book has taken quite a bit of time to finish. I became Academic Dean of Asia-Pacific Nazarene Theological Seminary in the middle of my writing, and my administrative responsibilities consumed most of my time. Much of the book was written during weekends. My wife Mary Ann, my daughter Heloise, and my son Jedidiah are God-sent sources of joy and inspiration; they keep me sane and motivated.

Now I am serving as Dean of the School of Leadership and Advanced Studies of Wesleyan University-Philippines, a higher education institution

Introduction

owned by the United Methodist Church. My work here has further deepened my understanding of divine grace. God is quick in forgiving our iniquities, and he is also generous is entrusting us his work and enabling us to fulfill his calling. The world is the scope of God's redemptive work, and here at the university, with the emphasis on environmental care and the United Nations' Sustainable Development Goals of President and retired Judge Benjamin D. Turgano, I see more clearly that the saving work of grace is truly cosmic and comprehensive.

1

Unmerited Beginnings

> "The earth is filled with your love, LORD"
>
> —PSALM 119:64

"In the beginning, God created the heavens and the earth" (Gen 1:1). We gaze in awe at the wonders and mystery of what God made. We are mesmerized by the beauty of sunsets, the serenity of forests, the whispers of cool breeze, the abundance of species, and the astonishing creativity of humans. Both the telescopic gaze at celestial bodies and the microscopic peek at the smallest particles cause us to exclaim: "Lord, our Lord, how majestic is your name in all the earth!" (Ps 9:1). When we are welcomed by the sight of dancing leaves swaying in the wind or illuminated by sunlight peering through the clouds, we are filled with gratitude to our Creator's generosity.

Our Gracious Creator

God is unique in his being. Speaking through the prophet Isaiah, God declares: "I am the Lord, that is my name, my glory I give to no other" (Isa 42:8). God stands over and above creation. He is transcendent. There is only God the Creator; everything else is creation. Even with its beauty and splendor recognized and celebrated, it is not God, and is never to be treated as such. To do so is to commit idolatry. The Bible repeatedly warns against giving to creation the praise and worship that belongs to God alone (Ps 135:15–18; Isa 41:7–10; 44:9–20).

All existence "declare[s] the glory of God" (Ps 19:1; 8:1), "proclaim[s] his righteousness" (Ps 50:6), and reveals his unmerited and boundless love. Creation reveals God's lavish generosity. Theologian Michael Lodahl observes that John Wesley's distinct contribution in reading Genesis is that he grounds God's creativity in love.[1] In this book we will use the same interpretive lens. God's love is self-giving and receptive of others. He is not threatened by creating things other than himself. As testimony to his love, God creates and then blesses his opposite. He creates "others" who can reciprocate in love. To speak of God creating in love is to speak of his grace. From beginning to end, the Bible is all about God's unmerited self-giving, whether by initially creating and then preserving the world, or in new creation (salvation) and its consummation. God creates freely, simply because he wants to, not out of necessity or in submission to some moral principles. If there were no creation, God would still be God in all his majesty, glory, and beauty. Creation neither adds to nor subtracts from God (Acts 17:25). Creaturely life results from divine freedom, unmerited love.

The Bible's affirmation of God as Creator should silence all who think of creation as inherently evil. This error was propagated by Marcion of Sinope (c. 85–160) who held that the Bible presents two radically different "Gods." The Old Testament God created the material word which is inherently and inescapably evil. This God is then opposed by the loving and gracious God of love seen in Jesus of Nazareth and in the Holy Spirit in the New Testament. The good God is the author of grace; the evil God is the author of law. Marcion and all his allies were wrong. There is one God, the holy God of love and grace (Ps 86:15). Love and grace mark everything he does. Marcion's contrast between the wrathful Creator Father and the gracious redeemer Jesus Christ fails to consider that creation is the work of the Triune God. The Father creates through the Word, the Son (John 1:3, 10; 1 Cor 8:6; Col 1:16; Heb 1:1—2:8). The Spirit breathes life upon creatures (Gen 2:7). The psalmist spells this trinitarian truth: "By the *word* of the Lord the heavens were made, their starry host by the *breath* of his mouth" (Ps 33:6, italics mine).

---

1. Lodahl, *God of Nature and of Grace*, 55.

Dependent Creaturely Existence

God continues his work in creation. In Christ all creation "holds together" (Col 1:17). Earthly existence is fickle. A massive solar storm could hit the earth and our technology would be wiped out. The entire planet could go dark. Tectonic plates often shift, setting off earthquakes and tsunamis that destroy human life and property. We believe that terrestrial life is dependent upon God's sustaining presence and activity. This is an affirmation of our faith in God the Creator. In the Nicene-Constantinopolitan Creed Christians affirm: "I believe in the Holy Spirit, the Lord and Giver of life." Merely to be alive is a gift. God "gives breath to its people" (Isa 42:5); withdrawal of this gift entails death (Job 34:14–15; Ps 104:29). The unmerited grace of the Creator is this: "The God who made the world and everything in it is the Lord of heaven and earth . . . And he is not served by human hands, as if he needed anything. Rather, he himself gives everyone life and breath and everything else" (Acts 17:24–25).

God's sustaining grace can be illustrated by a king who laboriously creates a kingdom. He would not then abandon it and allow it to fall into ruin. He would work to maintain its existence and prosperity. Similarly, God did not create the world, and then leave it to operate on its own. God is providentially present in his creation. He is a responsible God. Just as a mother who after giving birth spares no effort to sustain her child, God sustains his creation. The Calvinist theological tradition uses the term "common grace" to describe God's providence. The term means that God's sustaining care is directed toward every dimension and corner of his creation. The Bible supports this claim. "The Lord is good to all," the psalmist wrote, "he has compassion on all he has made" (Ps 145:9). "He has shown kindness," Paul told the citizens of Lystra, by "giving you rain from heaven and crops in their seasons; he provides you with plenty of food and fills your heart with joy" (Acts 14:17). Through his Son, the Father "created the world," and through his Son "he sustains all things by his powerful word" (Heb 1:1–4). God provides sunlight and rain to all (Matt 5:45; Job 37:13; Ps 65:9), including basic necessities of life such as food, water, and shelter (Gen 27:28; Ps 65:9; 104:14). He cares for each creature, even feeding birds and clothing flowers with splendor (Matt 6:26, 30). God's hands continue to tend the earth, like a gardener cherishing an ongoing project.

Grace and Salvation

God's rest on the seventh day symbolizes his contentment with his creation, not the termination of his creative involvement.[2] Old Testament scholar John H. Walton compares the Genesis language with Ancient Near East's creation stories where the Sabbath signifies the rest that follows after "a crisis has been resolved or when stability has been achieved."[3] In days one through six God created order out of disorder, life out of formlessness and void, and beauty out of chaos (Gen 1:1–2). On the seventh day, having achieved his purposes, God ceased to create. *Shabat* (Sabbath) "involves engagement in the normal activities that can be carried out when stability has been achieved."[4] In the Ancient Near East, for a deity to take rest means that he or she rests in a temple, and only in a temple. The temple signifies the center of the created order, the "control room" from which the deity rules. Therefore, when Yahweh rested on the seventh day, he was mounting his throne, taking command, and maintaining order in his creation.[5]

The Gift of Goodness

Thomas Aquinas, the most prominent theologian of the Middle Ages, taught that because creation is the product of God's good nature and will, it contains vestiges of God's qualities. God is like an artist who impresses upon a painting marks of his own characteristics. Paul indicated this when he said that through creation, "God's invisible qualities—his eternal power and divine nature—have been clearly seen" (Rom 1:20). Because God is good (1 Chr 16:34; Ps 31:19–20; 34:8; 100:4–5; 107:1; 136:1; Mark 10:18), his creation is good. "You are good," the psalmist wrote, "and what you do is good" (Ps 119:68). When Moses requested to see God's glory, his response was "I will cause all my goodness to pass in front of you" (Exod 33:18–19). The goodness of creation is like God's act of passing before our eyes, revealing—however dimly—the glory of the Creator.

---

2. Brueggemann, *Genesis*, 37.
3. Walton, *The Lost World of Genesis One*, 72.
4. Walton, *The Lost World of Genesis One*, 73.
5. Walton, *The Lost World of Genesis One*, 74.

Unmerited Beginnings

Open and Inviting Communion

The creation has a beginning; God does not. But this should not be taken to mean that God was a lone, solitary entity, something like the Unmoved Moved described by the Greek philosopher Aristotle. Instead, Triune life should be understood as a Communion of Love.[6] As Triune—one God who is Father, Son, and Holy Spirit—there is an eternal dynamism characterized by perfect community. Leonardo Boff is correct: "Community is the deepest and most fundamental reality that exists."[7] And it exists supremely as love in the Trinity. Triune Communion is perfect, requiring no external aid for completion. The eternal Triune communion is characterized by a term used by the early church fathers: *perichoresis*. It refers to the mutual indwelling and self-giving of the three Persons.[8] The Definition of the Council of Florence (concluded in 1445) explained: "the Father is totally in the Son and totally in the Spirit. The Son is totally in the Father and totally in the Spirit. The Holy Spirit is totally in the Father, totally in the Son."[9] *Perichoresis* means that the three Persons give themselves in selfless love, so much so that each Person is both *indwelling* and *room-giving* at the same time.

God, therefore, is Love (1 John 4:8). However, it is not enough to speak of God as Love; he is Holy Love. God's holiness establishes the nature of his love; his love establishes the character of his holiness. Here lies one of the mysteries of God's being. God's holiness entails his distinction from and transcendence above all creation. "I am the Lord," Yahweh proclaims, "and there is no other" (Isa 45:5). In the words of Rudolph Otto, he is "wholly Other." But his otherness must not be understood as remoteness. There is a boundary between God and creation in terms of being, but not in relationship. In fact, God's holiness is characterized by steadfast or faithful love in relationship (Hebrew *hesed*).[10] The Triune God who is holy love and who does not choose to stand aloof freely calls humans into covenantal communion with him. As Holy Love, God "is free to go outside of himself, and to share in the life of his creatures and enable them to share in his own

---

6. Torrance, *Trinitarian Perspectives*, 3.

7. Boff, *Holy Trinity*, 4.

8. The Latin translation of *perichoresis* was first *circumincessio*, then later *circuminsessio*. The former speaks of a dynamic interpenetration (*incedere*) and the latter of a lasting and resting mutual indwelling (*insedere*).

9. Quoted in Moltmann, "Perichoresis: An Old Magic Word for a New Trinitarian Theology," 114.

10. Greathouse, *Wholeness in Christ*, 21–22.

eternal Life and Love."[11] Therefore, it is not enough to say that God is a *Communion*. The Trinity, Jürgen Moltmann observes, is "an open, inviting, uniting, and integrating community . . ."[12] which is "open for its own sending . . . open for men and for all creation . . . open to the world and open to time."[13] Creation is the evidence of God's outflowing and overflowing love. God creates "the different" not for the sake of highlighting his transcendent Otherness, but to expand the already perfect Communion that he is. Our gracious God is a relation-making God.

The Gift of Life

Human existence as such falls far short of God's intention. To be merely alive for the sake of being alive is not God's ultimate design for humanity. The Greek word *zoe* ("life") means "fullness." It is related to the Hebrew word *shalom*, which means "whole-being" or "wholeness." To live truly, therefore, is to experience wholeness, enjoyment, or blessedness. This happens only in relationships, primarily with God. God declared that it is not good for humans to be alone (Gen 2:18). Humans were placed in the abundant Garden of Eden where they could experience life in its fullness. As a student in elementary school, I learned how interrelated life on earth is. Nothing exists simply for itself and by itself. Animals produce the carbon dioxide necessary for plant life and plants produce the oxygen required for animal life. All things exist in symbiotic relationships. This truth is theologically suggestive: God so designed life as to make it possible and enjoyable only in relationship with others. Experiencing true life is dependent on several intricate relations.

First, *we are created to be in intimate relationship with God*. "This is eternal life," Jesus said, "that they know you, the only true God" (John 17:3). This is not simply a relationship of dependency, but an open, dynamic, and reciprocal interaction. Walking with God is one of the early ways the Bible describes humankind's relationship with God. God placed Adam and Eve in the Garden where he could walk and dialogue with them. Enoch walked in fellowship with God without ever having to hide (Gen 5:21–24). The same was true for Noah (Gen 6:8–9). The purpose of God's call to Abraham was so that he would "walk" blamelessly before him. To walk with someone

11. Torrance, *Trinitarian Perspectives*, 2.
12. Moltmann, "Perichoresis," 117.
13. Moltmann, *The Church in the Power of the Spirit*, 55.

is to go in the same direction. The farther we walk with people, such as my journey with my wife, the more we get to know them and grow closer with them. Human life itself should be a journey of intimate friendship with God, "walking in obedience to him" (Deut 8:6). Just as God abounds in love toward us (Ps 86:15), we are to love him with all our heart, soul, body, and strength (Matt 22:37; Mark 12:30; Luke 10:27). Created by God and for God, we are meant to be with God. We are created to become God's conversation partners (Gen 1:28–30; 2:16–17). We are enabled to respond in obedience (Noah, Gen 6:13–21; Abraham, 12:1–3), in rebellion (Adam and Eve, Gen 3:9–19; Cain, 4:6–7, 9–15), or in dismay and exasperation (Ps 22:1–2; Hab 1:2–4). God asks questions to us and we in turn are permitted to raise questions to him (Ps 10:1; 13:1). Such is the grace of our Creator; he invites and enables us to be his conversation partners. This is both a privilege and a responsibility. God created humans in his own image; we are able and free to love. Although our relationship with God is asymmetrical because God always gives more, in love we share in God's own character that embraces "the different" or "the other."

Second, *God designed humans to live in harmonious relationship with creation.* Because we humans believe we are special in God's sight, we often forget that we are part of the created order. God placed Adam and Eve in the Garden not only to walk with God, but to enjoy sustained earthly life (Gen 2:9). The fullness of life in all its dimensions—material, religious, economic, emotional, and social—can be experienced in God's good creation. True, we owe our continued existence to God's providence, but he accomplishes this through his creation. Of course, life in God's creation is reciprocal. Creation provides for us. But we are also instructed to take care of the earth. Adam and Eve were placed in the Garden not only to eat of it, but also "to work and take care of it" (Gen 2:15). God gave us *permission* to consume the fruits of the earth (Gen 1:29–30; 2:16) and the *vocation* to be its royal gardeners (Gen 2:15).[14] Fullness of life can only be enjoyed in stewardly relationship.

The constitution of our human-ness reveals a two-fold orientation, one toward God and the other towards the world. We are creatures made from the dust of the ground. This highlights our intrinsic relationship with creation. But we are also creatures given life by the breath of God (Gen 2:7). Although we are formed from humble material, we are also exalted as bearers of the image of God (Gen 1:26–27). Both of these require

---

14. Brueggemann, *Genesis*, 48.

balance. On the one hand, some are tempted to focus on God and forget their earthliness. On the other hand, others are so preoccupied with their relationship with creaturely realities they forget their responsibility to God. Both dimensions are required of us. We are related to the world as God's priests. God created the world as a temple where humankind could fulfill its priestly vocation of not only representing God to creation and creation to God, but also in acting as God's servants in keeping creation.[15]

Third, *we are created to be in loving relationship with other humans.* Even when Adam was in an unbroken relationship with God and creation in the Garden, he was lonely. The company of animals was not sufficient (Gen 2:19–20). Something was missing. It seems that to be in relationship with God and creation is not enough to experience true life or wholeness. Indeed, "it is not good for the man to be alone" (Gen 2:18), God recognized. We need our fellow human beings. In response to Adam's loneliness, the Creator said, "I will make a helper suitable for him" (Gen 2:18). In some contexts the English word "helper" has negative connotations. In Asia and Middle East, to be a "helper" is to occupy a low social status. A helper is one who is assumed to be less educated and who works as someone's maid. This is thus used in some contexts to justify the social demotion of women. Contrary to this, the Hebrew word *ezer* not only nullifies female oppression, it exalts women to equality with men. The term refers not to a weaker person serving a superior, but to assisting someone in need. In fact, Joseph Coleson argues that *ezer* must be translated as "strength" or "power" or "autonomous being." The woman was equal with Adam in every sense. Eve's creation shows the importance of women, not their inferiority. This is confirmed by the following word—*negdo*—which means "equal and adequate." Therefore, instead of a relationship of superiority and inferiority, the intended relationship between Adam and Eve was one of mutual respect, admiration, and love.

Coleson's translation of Genesis 2:18 is worth quoting in full: "To end the loneliness of the single human, I will make another power, another autonomous being, like it, corresponding to it, of the same species, and facing it, standing opposite it in an equal I-Thou relationship, another human, its equal."[16] Adam and Eve equally bear the image of God (Gen 1:26–27). Both are given the commandment to become stewards of creation (Gen 1:28).

---

15. Walton, *The Lost World of Genesis One*, 77–85; Walton, *The Lost World of Adam and Eve*, 88–90.

16. Coleson, *"Ezer Cenegdo,"* 14.

The first humans were called to live in harmony, openness, and honesty. This is indicated in Genesis 2:25, "Adam and his wife were both naked, and they felt no shame." Their nakedness symbolizes their openness and trust. There was no malice, no need to protect themselves against each other, and no need to establish boundaries.

Cosmic Covenant

The invitation to relationship with God is not given exclusively to humans. We might be the crown of creation, but this does not mean the rest of creation is less important. We must not project onto God our notions regarding hierarchy and levels of superiority. Granted, humans play a special role in creation, as Psalm 8:4–8 declares:

> What is mankind that you are mindful of them,
> human beings that you care for them?
> You have made them a little lower than the angels
> and crowned them with glory and honor.
> You made them rulers over the works of your hands;
> you put everything under their feet:
> all flocks and herds, and the animals of the wild,
> the birds in the sky, and the fish in the sea,
> all that swim the paths of the seas.

Nevertheless, this does not mean that God's concern is exclusively for humans. The so-called "anthropic principle," if interpreted to imply that the whole created order revolves around humans, needs to be evaluated. This is simply not true. God is the center of creation, and no creature must assume God's place. The place of humans in creation is paradoxical. As assigned by God, humans are meant to be royal priests who bear God's image and represent him to the world. They are also stewards of creation and they bear an image not assigned to the rest of creation. But Genesis 1:26–28 does not mean that God grants preferential treatment to humans over other creatures. God also cares for the whole created order. The Spirit hovered over the waters, beautifying the chaotic cosmos (Gen 1:1–2). He planted a garden (Gen 2:8) where he takes a stroll (Gen 3:8). In forming Adam, God interacted with dirt and mud (Gen 2:7) like a master craftsman (Ps 139:13–14; Job 38:14). In the same way he cares for humans, God provides food and guidance for animals (Ps 104:21, 27–29; Matt 6:26–30). Just as humans are recipients of God's laws, he instilled order in the universe. He employs the service of animals, like ravens bringing food to Elijah (1 Kgs 17:4–6). Creation worships (Ps 104:18–24; 148:7–10; Job 38:25–27; 39:5–8; 39:26—40:2) in response to divine invitation: "Let everything that has breath praise the Lord" (Ps 150:6). We need to affirm the integrity and dignity of all creation. The covenant God established with Noah was inclusive of "all living creatures on earth" (Gen 9:8). God values the life of creatures because they belong to him (Ps 50:10–11). God's love is cosmic. His covenant is universal (Gen 9:8–17). This provides the background for the hope of new creation so central to the New Testament, and for the affirmation made by Paul that the whole creation, negatively affected by Adam's sin, will be redeemed (Rom 8:18–25).

Conclusions

The creation story brings us back to the very beginning of world and salvation histories. Genesis narrates God's love story with his creation. We are prepared to understand the miracle of forgiveness, transformation, and new creation because we know how graciously God acted in the beginning. Our gracious Maker is also our gracious Redeemer: "For your Maker is your husband—the Lord Almighty is his name—the Holy One of Israel is your Redeemer; he is called the God of all the earth" (Isa 54:5). So God's grace in creation is continuous with his grace in redemption. God's love is the foundation for both. The creation narrative is not only interested in the narration of facts; it spells many things about our existence on earth and about who the Creator God is as a magnanimous donor and sustainer of life and beauty, capable of creating "the different other" and inviting them to intimate relationship with him. We live in the contexts of our obedient standing before God, our reciprocal mutuality with others, and our vocation as stewards of and within creation. God's gift of life is meant to be enjoyed in this three-fold relationship. The purposes he instituted for creation remain unchanged. His redemptive action that culminates in the cross is in continuity with Genesis. This is the dignity of creation as the object of God's love and grace.

2

Mystery of Iniquity

> "The Lord God banished him from the Garden of Eden to work the ground from which he had been taken"
>
> —GENESIS 3:23

READING THE FIRST CHAPTERS of Genesis is like being at a concert where an orchestra is playing a beautiful symphony. The musical instruments are all tuned with each other, hitting their notes perfectly. There is a grand solemn atmosphere as the musical score narrates a journey mixed with passion and excitement. As everyone's attention is held captive by the crescendo that inspires feelings of glory and majesty, a blackout occurs. Human noise suddenly overwhelms the musical instruments. Previous feelings of enthusiastic appreciation are immediately forgotten, replaced by confusion, resentment, and anger. The dramatic turn of events is abrupt. This is the story of humanity in grace and sin. Because Genesis 1 to 12 presents a universal story, it also explains the presence of sin. It answers questions such as: What happened to God's good creation and to God's design for relationship? What happened to the man-woman union in a world of separations? What happened to the abundance and beauty of creation in a world full of disorder?

Grace and Salvation

The Nature of Sin

The story of God's grace is not perfectly rose-colored from beginning to end. It transparently includes episodes of human failure. The introduction of a talking serpent in Genesis 3 indicated a new beginning in the whole narrative (Gen 3:1). If God was the architect of goodness and dignity, the serpent was the pioneer of evil and sower of disorder.[1] Unfortunately, the serpent accomplished its goal.

Undermining God's Being

Lodahl aptly asserts that sin involves "a shifting of attention from the Creator to the creature" and is "a matter of asserting self-sovereignty against the divine."[2] The root of the problem was that the Adam and Eve, consciously or unconsciously, welcomed a third party into the God-human relationship. God gave humanity the dignity to be his conversation partner, and he intended that we talk *with* him. The serpent, however, diverted the conversation so that humans talk *about* him. God and his words became the subjects of conversation, scrutiny, and judgment. The serpent's first and second statements, "Did God really say, 'You must not eat from any tree in the garden'"? (Gen 3:1) and "God knows that when you eat from it your eyes will be opened, and you will be like God, knowing good and evil" (Gen 3:5) question God's generous grace. God became an unreasonable thrift, withholding from humanity what appears to be basic human rights. The serpent also opposed God's statements about the consequence of disobedience: "You will not certainly die" (Gen 3:4). It presented God as the enemy of human progress and who manipulates human freedom using untruthful threats. It attacked God's good will and proved from the prohibition of eating that God's will toward humans is questionable. The serpent, on the other hand, presented itself as a generous benefactor that sets humans free.

---

1. In the New Testament, the serpent is referred to as the devil (John 8:44; 2 Cor 11:3, 14; Rev 12:9; 20:2). Walton argues that the serpent in the story, if understood in Ancient Near Eastern perspective, refers to a chaos creature whose mission is to sow disorder through "deception, misdirection, and troublemaking." See *The Lost World of Adam and Eve*, 134.

2. Lodahl, *The Story of God*, 78.

Undermining God's Word

God's prohibition was given as a command: "You *must* not eat from the tree of the knowledge of good and evil" (Gen 2:17), but the serpent relegated it as a casual statement. God did not just say; God commanded. Moreover, it turned God's single prohibition to a general prohibition (compare Gen 2:16–17 and Gen 3:1). This strategy is an example of *awah*, one of the Hebrew terms used to depict sin in the Old Testament (Prov 12:8; Isa 19:14). It literally means "to bend or twist" the words of God so that they fit our preference or situation. The serpent's next statements became blatant oppositions to God. "You will not certainly die," the serpent argued, and then continued, "God knows that when you eat from it your eyes will be opened, and you will be like God" (Gen 3:4–5). In three statements, the serpent distorted God's words (Gen 3:1), denied the truthfulness of God's words (Gen. 3:4), and denied the consequences of disobedience to God's words (Gen 3:5).[3]

Undermining God's Designs

The most appealing part of the serpent's promise was that humans "will be like God, knowing good and evil" (Gen 3:5). The serpent's lectures and interpretation perhaps flabbergasted her, tickled her curiosity, and confirmed that she was a frog in a well who can only see a piece of the sky. She felt very little because the serpent seemed to be more knowledgeable than her. To merely eat the fruit, which was also "good for food and pleasing to the eye," and immediately "be like God, knowing good and evil" sounded like a great bargain. Adam and Eve desired a status in creation beyond what God awarded humans. They became discontent about human finitude. They desired to make themselves the co-center of order and co-source of wisdom, and to share in God's rightful place in his own creation.[4] Instead of remaining dependent and obedient, in the words of William Ernest Henley's poem *Invictus*, they wanted to be the master of their fates and the captain of their souls. Bonhoeffer's comparison between humans in the image of God and humans like God is worth quoting in length:

> *Imago dei*—Godlike man in his existence for God and neighbor, in his primitive creatureliness and limitation; *sicut deus*—Godlike man in his out-of-himself knowledge of good and evil, in

---

3. Emmrich, "The Temptation Narrative," 9–16.
4. Walton, *The Lost World of Adam and Eve*, 141–48.

his limitlessness and his acting out-of-himself, in his underived existence, in his loneliness. *Imago dei*—that is, man bound to the Word of the Creator and living from him; *sicut deus*—that is, man bound to the depths of his own knowledge about God, in good and evil; *imago dei*—the creature living in the unity of obedience; *sicut deus*—the creator-man living out of the division of good and evil.[5]

Humans are created to feel, live, and act in finitude. Possessing limitations and being dependent on God are constituents of our creatureliness. The problem is self-idolatry. Bonhoeffer added: "The word 'disobedience' does not exhaust the facts of the case. It is revolt, it is the creature's departure from the attitude which is the only possible attitude for him, it is the creature's becoming Creator, it is the destruction of creatureliness. It is defection; it is the fall from being held in creatureliness."[6]

Godlikeness is approved by God. God admonished his people to reflect his holiness (Lev 11:44–45; 19:2; 20:7; 1 Pet 1:16) and be perfect like him (Matt 5:48). We are called to imitate God (Eph 5:1) and are commanded to be like Christ (John 13:13–15; 1 Cor 11:1; Phil 2:5–8; 1 Pet 2:21; 1 John 2:6). Our goal is to be "transformed into [Christ's] likeness with ever-increasing glory" (2 Cor 3:18). The problem lies in the means toward godlikeness. God dictates the pace of our knowledge of him in accordance with our intimate relationship with him. Relationship precedes knowledge and godlikeness. The first humans wanted to achieve godlikeness—which was God's plan all along for them—behind his back and outside of his appointed time.

The serpent used godlikeness on the surface as a bait, but its hidden intention is really god-separatedness. The serpent's use of *Elohim*, instead of God's covenant name *Elohim Yahweh* (how God is primarily addressed in Genesis 2:4—3:24, underscoring creation's covenant relationship with the Creator) reveals at least two things. First, the serpent intentionally detached itself from God, reflecting its alienation from him. Second, the

---

5. Bonhoeffer, *Creation and Fall*, 71.

6. Bonhoeffer, *Creation and Fall*, 76. Otto J. Baab, expresses human sin well: "Man is God's creature, made of the dust of the ground but in the likeness of God. Man is weak, mortal, but aspiring. He seeks to exercise power, thus to be like God and to forget his creatureliness. So he builds his civilizations, his cities, his Towers of Babel. He sets up the idols of his mind and heart, allowing these to replace the God who is his Creator and Provider. This is his sin—his deliberate, sustained effort to deny the God of his life by glorifying the work of his own hands and brain. Man rebelliously turns to the pursuit of political power, economic wealth, national pre-eminence, even to the creeds and ceremonies of religion, in an endeavor to escape the demands of humility and obedience which are made by his God." See Baab, "The God of Redeeming Grace," 133.

serpent intentionally removed the covenantal relationship between God and humans from the woman's consciousness in the course of the conversation. The success of its schemes rested on this. Its agenda was not only to create a wedge between God and humans but to proselyte others in joining its lonely alienation.

Sadly, like Adam and Eve, we fail to recognize what is truly best for us. Baited by thoughts of gains, our relationship with God is sacrificed. Our alienation from God stems from our own short-sightedness. The greatest temptations are related to real human needs. A thief covets someone else's property because he has a family to feed. A woman prostitutes herself because of her need of companionship. A small-time businessman cheats because he needs financial security. A nation wages war against another because of the pursuit of peace. The examples can go on. Humans commit sin and risk alienation from God for pragmatic benefits. The temptation that led to human demise is the basic act of eating! People stupidly choose short-term and modest gains at the cost of what really matters: intimate relationship with God.

The Wages of Sin

The covenant relationship between God and humans in the Garden was entirely God's initiative, but its condition for continuation rested on humanity's obedience. Genesis 1–3 can be summarized in the words of Paul: "The wages of sin is death but the gift of God is eternal life" (Rom 6:23). In a sense, the serpent was right, because the first humans did not immediately die. Adam lived for 930 years (Gen 5:5). Nevertheless, human death became certain when God pronounced that humanity "must not be allowed to reach out his hand and take also from the tree of life and eat, and live forever" (Gen 3:22). The pronounced death, of course, was both physical (Rom 7:2–3; 8:36) and spiritual (Prov 23:14; Rom 6:16, 21, 23; 7:5, 9–11, 24; 8:2, 6). In Greek thought, *thanatos* ("death") literally means the separation between the body and the soul. The idea of separation is important, because the consequence of sin is separation in three levels: from God, from each other, and from creation. Sin is a relational term; its consequences therefore are also broken relationships and distorted love.

Grace and Salvation

Alienation from God

If the dignity of humanity is grounded in intimate communion with God, the degradation of humanity is found in the distortion and loss of this communion. The primary consequence of sin is spiritual death. John Wesley wrote: "The moment [Adam] tasted that fruit he died. His soul died, was separated from God."[7] The unmediated conversations in Genesis 1–2 underscore the unbroken relationship between God and humanity. The Garden was a place of life and intimacy; God was depicted as "walking in the garden in the cool of the day" (Gen 3:8). Humanity's natural habitat was also God's dwelling place.

The act of hiding from God was completely out of place (Gen. 3:8). Sin made God's mere presence a source of dread and anxiety. We can easily understand this. A thief feels uncomfortable in the presence of a policeman, whether or not the policeman knows of his crimes. There is a great sense of relief when the policeman leaves the premises. Alienation is not imposed by God to us; it is the immediate response of sinners to hide from God's presence. We alienate ourselves from him; not the other way around. Peter voiced this out perfectly: "Go away from me Lord, for I am a sinful man!" (Luke 5:8). In sin, we run away from God because of guilt and shame. Ironically, God's absence gives us a false sense of security. Adam provided the reason why they hid: "I heard you in the garden, and I was afraid because I was naked" (Gen 3:10). The primeval delight is gone. They no longer saw God as a gracious giver, but as a judge-punisher. Their perspectives about themselves also changed. Fueled by self-preservation, they became self-centered: "I heard . . . , I was afraid . . . , I was naked . . . , I hid . . . , I ate . . ." (Gen 3:10–13). As Murray Lightenstein wrote: "In their shame, they are now self-related. Focused on their own individuality and isolation, they are painfully aware of their creatureliness, of the 'incongruity' involved in the creature-Creator relationship."[8]

Genesis 3 portrayed God as a Questioner. The Garden was supposedly a place of enjoyment, but it became a court room. God, however, was not the only accuser. In the minds of humans, God also stood accused. When God asked Adam about his disobedience, he directly blamed "the woman *you* put here with me" (Gen 3:12, italics mine). When God asked the woman about her wrong, she had the same audacity to blame God for the

---

7. Wesley, "Justification by Faith," in *Works* (BE) 1: 185.
8. Lightenstein, "The Fearsome Sword of Genesis 3:24," 365.

existence of the serpent, which God created (Gen 3:13). Genesis 3:22–24 highlights the severity of the alienation. God "drove [them] out." Humanity wanted to hide from God in the Garden, so God completely banished them from it. This is profoundly symbolic. Being banished implies inaccessibility to abundance and being separated from God and his presence. This is what death truly means.

Social Fragmentation

The self-centeredness and self-preservation that ruined humanity's relationship with God also resulted in the fragmentation of human relationships. The moral and political aspects of the image of God in humanity were distorted. As soon as Adam and Eve made the "I" the center of their existence, the husband-wife relationship (constituting the most basic love relationship in society) regressed. Their attitudes toward each other changed. When they realized they were naked, "they sewed fig leaves together and made coverings for themselves" (Gen 3:7; contrast with Gen 2:25). The problem was not nakedness, but mistrust and fear. Like their attitude towards God, they felt the need to hide from each other.

As Bonhoeffer wrote, "nakedness is the essence of unity and of unbrokenness, of being for the other, of objectivity . . . Nakedness is the essence of the ignorance of the possibility of robbing the other of his right. Nakedness is revelation, nakedness believes in grace . . . Nakedness is innocence."[9] In sin, they lost confidence and began to suspect each other. They no longer wished to remain vulnerable to each other's penetrating gaze for fear of judgment, criticism, or even malicious intentions. They objectified themselves but also feared being objectified. Bonhoeffer is once again correct in saying that

> Shame is the expression of the fact that we no longer accept the other person as the gift of God. Shame expresses my passionate desire for the other person and the knowledge that belongs to it that the other person is no longer satisfied just to belong to me but desires something from me. Shame covers me before the other because of my own evil and of his evil, because of the division that has come between us. Where the one accepts the other as the companion given to him by God, where it is content with understanding himself as beginning from and ending in the other and

9. Bonhoeffer, *Creation and Fall*, 78–79.

> in belonging to him, man is not ashamed. In the unity of unbroken obedience man is naked in the presence of man, uncovered, revealing both body and soul, and yet he is not ashamed. Shame only comes into existence in the world of division.[10]

Moreover, Adam and Eve defended themselves at the expense of the other. Because of self-preservation, they abandoned their original roles to support one another. Adam, instead of acting as the woman's advocate before God, placed all the blame and burden upon her (Gen 3:12), although he was "with her" during the whole duration of the temptation (Gen 3:6).[11] Adam selfishly championed the concept of individual responsibility to exonerate himself of crime.

Finally, the relationship of equality was changed to that of mutual desire to dominate the other. God commissioned Adam to name animals (Gen 2:19–20), and in naming his own wife (Gen 3:20), he considered her as his possession and equal to animals. The description of God about the woman as *negdo* ("equal," Gen 2:20) was overruled by Adam's desire for superiority. The woman, in the name of justice, will retaliate and also seek to dominate her husband. When God said to Eve, "your desire will be for your husband" (Gen 3:16), this actually did not mean that Eve will silently submit to him. The Hebrew word used, *tesuqa*, occurs only twice in the Old Testament, and its usage in Genesis 4:7 is related to sin that seeks to rule over. The analogy is that of a lion patiently waiting for the prey's moment of weakness before devouring it whole. Unfortunately, God said that the man "will rule over you" (Gen 3:16). The woman will try to usurp her husband's dominion, but her husband will continue to be a tyrant. The once relationship of trust, equality, and mutual support turned to a relationship of dispute and domination.[12]

Frustration of Creation

God created the world for humanity, and vice versa. On the one hand, the Garden was filled with fruit-bearing trees, ready for humanity's consumption. On the other hand, well-fed humanity will also care for the land as royal priests. Unfortunately, this symbiotic relationship of mutual support

---

10. Bonhoeffer, *Creation and Fall*, 63.
11. See Parker, "Blaming Eve Alone," 729–47.
12. Hamilton, *The Book of Genesis Chapters 1–17*, 201–2.

and care was distorted by sin. The trees that were meant to sustain life became walls to isolate humans from God. This is death! Mutual support was replaced by mutual enmity, which will ultimately result in the serpent's death and the bruising of the woman's heels (Gen 3:15). They would bring pain and destruction upon each other. Humanity will abuse the earth. The image of toiling denotes the deformation of the soil in order to mine its nutrients and resources (Gen 3:17). Sadly, humanity has no choice but to do this if we are to survive. Trapped in a cycle, human sustenance and progress will necessitate ecological rape.[13]

God did not rescind his mandate for humans to be governors of creation (Gen 1:28), but humans will exercise this authority poorly. As corrupted stewards, we make judgments about what is good for us at the expense of creation. "The accepted cause of such devastation," Peter Heineqq writes, "is that it arises more or less inevitably from soaring numbers of hyperactive humans equipped with increasingly virulent technology, something like a gang of sorcerer's apprentices running amok with bulldozers instead of brooms."[14] Creation will respond in retaliation against humanity's abuse. As if angry at the incompetence of its appointed lords, creation will be thrifty in producing food for humanity's sustenance. God's pronounced punishments reveal this: "through painful labor you will eat food from it" (Gen 3:17), "you will eat the plants of the field" (Gen 3:18), and "by the sweat of your brow you will eat your food" (Gen 3:19). The soil will not only withhold abundant food; it will also "produce thorns and thistles" (Gen 3:18). "Agricultural production," Collins wrote, "is the arena of God's chastisement."[15] Creation has been truly subjected to frustration (Rom 8:20) because the ground is itself cursed on our account (Gen 3:17; 4:11; 5:29; Deut 28:17–18, 20, 38–46). God's punishment directed to humanity needed an agent, and creation itself was given this responsibility.

Universal Sin

We would like to think that the story of the Fall represents the lowest possible ebb of human history. Having learned important lessons the hard way, we expect better human performance outside the Garden. Sadly, the human predicament in sin continued to expand to catastrophic proportions.

13. Clemens, "The Law of Sin and Death," 6.
14. Heineqq, "The Ecological Curse," 445.
15. Collins, "What Happened to Adam and Eve?" 38.

Instead of reconciliation, humans took their alienation from God, from each other, and from creation to even greater levels. In Genesis 4, the fault no longer focuses on Adam and Eve but on their offspring. God's question to Cain, "If you do what is right, will you not be accepted?" (Gen 4:6) reveals that like his parents, he failed to reach the standard of obedience. Instead of confessing his faults, like his parents, he put the blame of his failure on to his brother Abel. Like his parents, he viewed his brother Abel as a competition who needed to be subdued. When intimidating Abel did not work, he retorted to murder. When confronted by God, Cain's response was a heartless remark that the welfare of others was none of his concerns: "Am I my brother's keeper?" (Gen 3:9). The essence of sin is self-centeredness.

The descendants of Adam and Eve followed in their footsteps. Several generations later, the human situation has reached shocking proportions that God could no longer "contend with man forever" (Gen 6:3). The divine evaluation was heart-breaking. Wickedness became universal in scope: "Now the earth was corrupt in God's sight and was full of violence. God saw how corrupt the earth had become, for all the people on earth had corrupted their ways" (Gen 6:11–12). Several generations after the flood, the cycle of sin and disobedience continued, evident in the construction of the tower of Babel (Gen 11:1–9). Like Adam and Eve who desired transcendence, self-centered humans tried to build "a tower that reaches to the heavens" so that they may "make a name" for themselves (Gen 11:4). Evil has become systemic that they collectively and unanimously agreed to go beyond the bounds of God-set human limitations. Like Adam and Eve, they were also concerned with self-preservation (Gen 11:4). The tower served as humanity's contingency plan should God decide to send another cosmic flood, so its erection entailed both disobedience and mistrust in God's covenant promises to Noah (see Gen 9:12–17). Ironically, the consequence of their united effort was scattering over all the earth (Gen 11:8). Sin resulted again in banishment.

Conclusions

The sharp turn of events in world history in the first chapters of the Bible is shocking. The transitions were from excessive abundance to gripping poverty, from careless enjoyment to worrisome suffering, from naked innocence to clothed maliciousness, from delightful God-centeredness to wanton self-centeredness, from exocentric existence to egocentric disposition, from symbiotic partnership to parasitical competition, from graceful openness to rabid privatization and individualism, and from life in relationship to death in separation. The human predicament is comprehensive and universal in scope. The biblical testimony is that "no one does good" (Ps 14:1, 3), there is "no one who does not sin" (1 Kgs 8:46; Rom 3:23), and "no one living is righteous" (Ps 143:2; Eccl 7:20; Rom 3:10–11). Everyone has sinned and fallen short of God's glory (Rom 3:23). Everyone is living under the power of sin (Rom 3:9). The corruption of humanity is comprehensive, affecting the body (Rom 6:6, 12; 8:10), the mind or reason (Rom 1:21; 2 Cor 3:14–15, 4:4), the emotions (Rom 1:26–27; Gal 5:24; 2 Tim 3:2–4), and the will ("slaves to sin," Rom 6:17; 2 Tim 2:25–26).[16]

Sadly, although we are aware of our predicament, we are unable to do anything about it (Eph 2:1–2, 5; Col 2:13; Heb 6:1; 9:14). Left on our own, even with our best efforts and well-planned schemes, we are unable to save ourselves. Only God can save us (Eph 2:8–9). "I am the Lord," God said, "and apart from me there is no savior" (Isa 43:11). The good news is that God's original design for humanity to enjoy life in abundance and communion never changed. He is capable of saving us, and he does act to save us. He does not leave us in our sin and death. He takes the initiative. This is what the next chapter is all about.

---

16. See Wesley's description of humanity corrupted by sin in "Sermon on the Mount I," in *Works* (BE) 1: 477–78. "There cannot be in any man," Wesley wrote, "one good temper or desire, or so much as one good thought," in "Advise to the People Called Methodists," in *Works* (BE) 9: 124–25.

3

One for the Many

> "I will make your name great, and you will be a blessing...
> and all peoples on earth will be blessed through you"
>
> —GENESIS 12:2–3

GOD'S MAGNANIMITY AND CREATION'S dignity are important themes in the first pages of history. Humans enjoyed harmonious communion with the Creator, with fellow humans as helpers and lovers, and with creation as companions and sustainers. We know, however, with great sorrow, that this beautiful state of affairs was ruined by sin. Concord was replaced by conflicts. Abundant prosperity was replaced by stifling poverty. Being-with-God was replaced by banishment. Instead of seeking to make things right with God, we are flabbergasted that the first humans continued to spiral down to depravity. From Genesis 3, the Bible became filled with conflict and tension. The situation got very bad that God decided to do a hard reboot through the flood. The fresh start is evident in the parallel statements in Genesis 1–2 and Genesis 9:

Genesis 1–2	Genesis 9
"Be fruitful and increase in number; fill the earth" (1:28)	"Be fruitful and increase in number and fill the earth" (9:1, 7)
"... subdue it. Rule over the fish of the sea and the birds of the air and over every living creature that moves on the ground" (1:28)	"all the beast of the earth and all the birds of the air ... every creature ... all fish ... they are given into your hands" (9:2)
"I give you every seed-bearing plant on the face of the whole earth and every tree that has fruit with seed in it. They will be yours for food. And all the beasts of the earth ..." (1:29)	"Everything that lives and moves will be food for you. Just as I have given you the green plants, I now give you everything" (9:3)
"But you must not eat from the tree of the knowledge of good and evil" (2:17)	"But you must not eat meat that has its lifeblood in it" (9:4)

The parallel between creatures emerging from what was once formless and void to populate the earth (Gen 1:1–31) and the emergence of animals from the ark after the flood as a result of God speaking (Gen 8:15–19), is unmistakable. A dove hovered over the flood waters (Gen 8:8–12) like the Spirit hovering over primeval creation (Gen 1:2). The flood story is the re-creation of the face of the earth. But the joy of re-creation is short-lived. Noah, the "righteous man" who "walked with God" (Gen 6:9) fell short. The theme of nakedness appears again, and Noah was angry for being exposed to his son Ham (Gen 9:21). He cursed his own son, revealing broken human relations again. The only unity humans enjoyed later was in their effort to "make a name" for themselves (Gen 11:4). Like in Adam and Eve's story, pride, self-centeredness, and self-preservation were humanity's downfall.[1]

Grace and Promise

Although humans always found ways to displease him, God remains gracious. Adam and Eve were given the opportunity to bring new life to the world (Gen 3:16). Although Cain's punishment was to be a wanderer, God protected him from hateful death (Gen 4:12, 15). Although Cain "went

---

1. In the story or Noah, we find the realization that the sustenance and redemption of creation is not predicated at all on the inherent goodness of creation found in Genesis 1–2. Rather they are acts of divine grace amidst human wickedness. See Rendtorff, "Covenant," 388.

out from the Lord's presence" (compare Gen 3:22–24 and 4:16), like his parents he was given progenies (Gen 4:17–19). Although God wiped out human life on earth, he gave humanity a fresh start through Noah and his family (Gen 6:1—9:17). When God was displeased at the construction of the tower of Babel, he scattered them to prevent further evil collaborations (Gen 11:1–9). God is determined to be gracious to his erring creation.

Garments of Skin

In the light of Adam and Eve, and Noah, nakedness, it seems, brings both fear and shame in relationships.[2] The first humans needed to be clothed. Thus, "the Lord God made garments of skin" (Gen 3:21). This simple verse spells several things about human salvation. First, the price to be paid to cover our shame is costly. Prefiguring temple sacrifices and ultimately Jesus Christ's death on the cross, at-one-ment with God entails the death of a sacrifice. Indeed, "without the shedding of blood there is no forgiveness" (Heb 9:22; cf. Lev 17:11). Second, at-one-ment implies being covered. This is what the Hebrew word for atonement—*kipper*—means: "to cover." We need to be covered and cleansed by the blood of the lamb. (We will look at the concept of covering more in detail in the next chapter.) Third, the sacrifice is initiated by God. Human ingenuity in sowing fig leaves was not sufficient (Gen 3:7). God had to intervene for a better and long-lasting solution. Fourth, the cost of reconciliation is borne by God himself. God suffers the pain of the death of the innocent for the sake of redemption.

Seed of the Woman

In Genesis 3:15, God declared that enmity will characterize the relationship between the serpent and the woman, which will carry on with their offspring. But a time will come when the woman's descendant will once and for all end this enmity, along with the consequence of sin. The question, however, is when? Eve expected the fulfillment to be immediate. She named her first-born Cain, meaning, "I have brought forth a man, *even the Lord*" (Gen 4:1).[3] We can easily understand Eve's longing for relief to come

---

2. In accordance to Jewish and Christian traditions, Parvan wrote, to be naked is to be in a shameful state. See her article "Genesis 1–3: Augustine and Origen on the Coats of Skins," 62.

3. Kaiser, *Mission in the Old Testament*, 16. Kaiser's translation is close to the

sooner than later. Cain, of course, was not God's appointed one. The promised seed may have been alluded to in Genesis 9:27 at the mention of the "tents of Shem," although again, the promised offspring was not any of the actual children of Shem. The theme of the chosen offspring emerged again in Genesis 12:1–3, where God promised Abraham that his progenies will become as numerous as the stars (Gen 15:5; 22:7; 26:4), and it is through them that all nations will be blessed (Gen 22:18). Of course, this refers to Jesus Christ, but our discussion of his work will have to wait until chapters 6 and 7.

Universal Story

Genesis 1–11 records universal history, beginning with creation (chapters 1–2), followed by how sin entered the whole world (chapters 3–4), how humanity grew in number (chapter 5), the punishment and renewal of the whole world (chapters 6–9), the table of nations (chapter 10), and the scattering of the people around the world (chapter 11). The transition to the story of Abraham in Genesis 12 is not accidental in the light of the universal scope of God's action. According to James Muilenburg, there are four major episodes in Genesis 1–11, each with elements of beauty, sin, punishment, and words of promise.[4] In table:

narrative	sin	punishment	promise
life in paradise (Gen 2:4—3:24)	the first disobedience	expulsion from the Garden	clothing for nakedness and promise of the offspring
the two brothers (Gen 4:1–16)	murder of a brother	exile to be a wanderer	protection
the flood (Gen 6:9—9:17)	increase of wickedness	the flood	covenant not to annihilate the world again
the building of the tower (Gen 11:1–9)	pride and self-reliance	scattering of the nations	?

---

translation of International Standard Version: "I have given birth to a male child—the Lord."

4. Muilenburg, "Abraham and the Nations," 389–90.

Grace and Salvation

Noticeably, only the fourth episode is missing a promise of grace. Thrice, as the consequence of sin, humans were exiled from their place of comfort. The scattering of the people is also repeated thrice in Genesis 11, emphasizing the drastic human condition (Gen 11:4, 8, 9). Fortunately, the hanging episode of Genesis 11 is followed by God's action in calling Abraham, the work of grace that completes the four grand narratives. Like the other episodes (except the second), the fourth revolves around a single human whose life and action would influence world history. This is what we mean by "the one for the sake of the many."

Particular and Universal

Against the background of the scattered peoples throughout the world, God summoned one particular human back to himself in relationship. God was undoing the scattering, because Abraham is called to be relocated to Canaan, a place that would later be described as a land flowing with milk and honey (Gen 12:1; Exod 33:3). God's design for humans to enjoy the fullness of life in a land of abundance and in relationship with him remained the same. With Abraham at the juncture, the effects of sin were being reversed by God. The contrast in living circumstances between fallen and blessed humanity is easily noticeable when we read Genesis 12 in the light of Genesis 11:27–32, the story of Terah (Abraham's father). Before the promise of blessings in Genesis 12, life is characterized by "premature death, barrenness, and a family journey that peters out. The brief story of Terah's family is also the only section in Genesis 1–11 where God is never mentioned."[5] The story of Terah symbolizes the human predicament apart from God. Terah desired to reach Canaan, but he finally settled and died in Haran (Gen 11:31–32). Abraham's story was a departure from Haran, a place of death and the absence of God, to Canaan, a place of abundant life and the presence of God.

God of Initiatives

In calling Abraham, life emerged from death as a consequence of God's speech. Just as life, beauty, and order materialized out of nothingness and chaos because God spoke (Gen 1) and just as human existence was given

---

5. von Rad, *Biblical Interpretations in Preaching*, 197.

another chance amidst the destructive flood because God called Noah (Gen 6–9), life and blessings were in God's mind when he called Abraham (Gen 12). God's initiative was an act of free grace. Abraham did not possess commendable qualifications worthy of divine attention. He was a member of a loose group of monads called Apiru, or the "dusty ones." His father Terah "worshipped other gods" (Josh 24:2). The family came from Ur of the Chaldeans, most probably referring to the city of Babylon. This means that Abraham's family has its origin with Babel, the archetype of rebellion against God (Gen 11:31).[6] God takes initiatives among the ungodly. To use Paul's arguments, Abraham must be understood in the same category that everyone is in—both Jews and Greeks—as under sin (Rom 3:9, 10, 23). He was unrighteous before he received God's promises. God's creative work and Abraham's transition from ungodliness to righteousness is by grace, so there is no room for boasting (Rom 3:27). In the words of S. J. Gathercole, "God's declaration of Abraham as righteous was not a descriptive word but the creative word of God who calls 'nonentities' into being as 'entities.'"[7] God's new creation dawns upon the whole world.[8]

Enacted Faith

Abraham may have been chosen by sheer grace, but he was not a passive recipient of righteousness. He had to obey God's command, in faith, to leave Haran and go to the land God will show him (Gen 12:1). This is rich with symbolism. For the Jewish philosopher Philo, in order for Abraham to be truly committed to God, he needed to leave his family and the Chaldean religious mindset. Leaving Ur and Haran implied leaving error in order to accommodate the truths of God. This was not easy. Muilenberg expressed Abraham's sacrifice beautifully:

> It is a heavy burden that Yahweh calls upon Abram to bear. He must separate himself from all the natural bonds which normally determine a man's existence. He must separate himself from his native land, from all the psycho-physical protections of the land of his fathers. He must separate himself from the elemental

---

6. Campbell, "Refusing God's Blessing," 277–78.
7. Gathercole, *Where Is Boasting?*, 243; McFarland, "Whose Abraham," 120.
8. Lee, "דָּרָב in Genesis 35:11," 471.

> solidarities of family and kin . . . He must sacrifice these stabilities and go forth to a land the name of which he is not even told.[9]

It is precisely because he went "as the Lord had told him" (Gen 12:4) and believed in God's seemingly outrageous promises that he was called righteous. "Abram believed the Lord," Genesis 15:6 says, "and [God] credited it to him as righteousness" (Rom 4:3). The writer of Hebrews emphasizes the centrality of faith in everything Abraham did:

> "By faith Abraham, when called to go to a place he would later receive as his inheritance, obeyed and went, even though he did not know where he was going" (Heb 11:8)

> "By faith he made his home in the promised land like a stranger in a foreign country" (Heb 11:9)

> "By faith Abraham, when God tested him, offered Isaac as a sacrifice" (Heb 11:17)

Abraham's response of faith is the pattern for everyone to imitate. "The words 'it was credited to him' were written not for him alone," Paul wrote, "but also for us, to whom God will credit righteousness—for us who believe in him" (Rom 4:23–24).[10] Abraham's faith was not mere intellectual assent; it was concrete and enacted. That the root word for "blessing" means "to bend the knee" implies that humility and submission are important responses to receiving God's favor.[11] Interestingly, in Jewish writings, Abraham was justified because of his obedience (1 Macc 2:51–52; Sir 4:19–21; Jub 15:1–32; 16:20–31). This does not need to be contrasted with justification by faith. James is correct: "faith by itself, if not accompanied by action, is dead" (2:17).

It must also be noted that Abraham was already proclaimed righteous (Gen 15:6) prior to his circumcision (Gen 17). Paul capitalized on this in Galatians 3 where he argued that the promise came before the law. In his epistle to the Romans, Paul was even more direct: "We have been saying that Abraham's faith was credited to him as righteousness. Under what circumstances was it credited? Was it after he was circumcised, or before? It was not after, but before!" (Rom 4:9–10). Circumcision, thus, functions merely as "a sign, a seal of the righteousness that he had by faith while he

---

9. Muilenburg, "Abraham and the Nations," 391.
10. See Jipp, "Rereading the Story of Abraham," 217–42.
11. Gordon, "Barak," 757.

was still uncircumcised" (Rom 4:11).[12] Paul's interpretation of Abraham is Christologically-conditioned, and he was equally concerned about Abraham's faith and ours in relation to being proclaimed righteous.

The Concept of Blessing

It is not hard to see the analogous experiences of Adam and Abraham. First, Adam was molded out of the dust of the ground (Gen 2:7) while Abraham was called from his family of barrenness and death (Gen 11:30–32). Second, God desired for both of them to enjoy abundant life in the land God chose. The parallel between the Garden of Eden (Gen 2:8–16) and Canaan as a land flowing with mild and honey (Exod 33:3) is intriguing. Third, both were given the command or promise of posterity (Gen 1:28; 15:5; 22:17; 26:4). They are the fathers of many. Fourth, both were given promises and commands to obey (Gen 1:28–30; 12:1–3). They were God's conversation partners. Both were called to obey God's words. Adam had to trust in God's wisdom in prohibiting the consumption of the fruit of the tree of knowledge and evil. Abraham had to trust and depend on the reliability of God's words in asking him to migrate to a foreign land. Finally, both received the blessings of God. Immediately upon the creation of humans, "God blessed them" (Gen 1:28). God's blessing to Abraham is more pronounced:

> I will make you into a great nation, and I will bless you;
> I will make your name great, and you will be a blessing.
> I will bless those who bless you, and whoever curses you I will curse;
> and all peoples on earth will be blessed through you (Gen 12:2–3).

What does it mean to be blessed? This is the key word in God's salvific initiative through Abraham.[13] Why is the concept of blessing so central in the biblical message of grace and salvation? In the Ancient Near East, Robert P. Gordon argued, "nothing was more important that securing the blessing of God in one's life or nation. All religious and superstitious peoples have actively sought the blessing of a specific deity or spirit, believing that this blessing will make them fertile, or prosper them, protect them, deliver them, heal them, preserve them, empower them, exalt them, favor them, or, possibly, bring about all the above . . . A blessed life was the ideal; a life

---

12. Pyne, "The 'Seed,' the Spirit, and the Blessings of Abraham," 216.
13. Bauckham, *Bible and Mission*, 28–29.

Grace and Salvation

without God's blessing was the ultimate nightmare."[14] Receiving blessings is so crucial that conflicts emerge because of it: between Esau and Jacob (Gen 27:1—28:14), between Jacob and the man from God (Gen 32:26-28), and between Balak and Balaam in relation to the armies of Israel (Num 22–24).

To bless someone is to speak well of them and their future. Blessings are always something said.[15] We see this in God blessing Adam and Eve (Gen 1:28-29) and Abraham (Gen 12:1-3), in Isaac blessing Jacob (Gen 27:27-29), and in Jacob blessing his sons (Gen 49:1-28). The importance of these utterances cannot be underestimated. In Hebrew mindset, to be blessed is to receive righteousness (Prov 10:6), material prosperity (Prov 10:22), and anything necessary for survival and well-being (Exod 23:25-26; Deut 7:12-15). Isaac lamented when he realized that Esau's rightful blessing was received by Jacob. Esau became hysterical: "Bless me—me too, my father! . . . Do you have only one blessing, my father? Bless me too, my father!" (Gen 27:34, 38).

David J. A. Clines argues that the Abrahamic blessing contains three promises: posterity, divine-human relationship, and land.[16] Genesis 1–11 reveals that humanity turned to wickedness, the divine-human relationship was broken because of sin, and the whole earth was cursed. God's action in Genesis 12 is his response to the failures of creation in the preceding chapters. However, God's initiative must not be seen as a divine afterthought. Instead, God's promises in Genesis 12 are a return to his plans for humanity revealed in Genesis 1–2. God's design for humans to multiply in number, to be in harmonious relationships with him, with others, and with creation, and to experience life in abundance remained the same.

The promise of posterity is important because it is the direct opposite of the punishment of sin: death. The first divine commission was to reproduce (Gen 1:28). Adam and Eve were told, however, that if they disobey, they will die (Gen 2:17). It is no coincidence that the first promise to Abraham ("I will make you into a great nation," Gen 12:2) runs parallel the first divine command to Adam and Eve ("Be fruitful and increase in number," Gen 1:18). "The blessing that confers the power of fertility is inseparable from creation where the creator is the one who blesses and the created

---

14. Gordon, "Barak," 758.

15. Rotenberry, "Blessing in the Old Testament," 35.

16. Clines, *The Theme of the Pentateuch*, 31; cited in Davis, "Who are the Heirs of the Abrahamic Covenant?" 153.

living being has the power to reproduce itself because of the blessing."[17] The redemptive note of the promise of posterity is discernible in the Greek word *nekrosin*, which Paul used to describe Abraham (Rom 4:19). It is out of his already dead body that life springs. There is hope for humanity, because God wills that death is not the final word.

Second, the calling of Abraham symbolizes the restoration of the broken relationship between God and humanity. The tragic consequence of sin is shame. As such, human initiative in approaching God for reconciliation in humility and confession is a pipe dream. God approached Abraham in the same way that he looked for Adam and Eve in the Garden (Gen 3:9). Abraham was promised a "great name" (Gen 12:2), which implies being found pleasing in his sight (see Abraham, Gen 17:5; Israel, Gen 32:28; Peter, John 1:42; Jesus, Phil 2:9). In Abraham, God was restoring humanity to their proper standing before him in blessed relationship. Moreover, in his covenant with Abraham, God also promised a land where humans can enjoy life: "The whole land of Canaan, where you now reside as a foreigner, I will give as an everlasting possession to you and your descendants after you; and I will be their God" (Gen 17:7–8). This promise is given to Abraham (Gen 12:5–7; 13:13–17; 15:7–18, 19–21), Isaac (Gen 26:3–4), and Jacob (Gen 28:3, 13–15; 35:9–12). The possession of land is both physical and theological. God was undoing human banishment from the Garden (Gen 3:22–24) and the scattering of people (Gen 11) by allocating a land specifically where his people will gather and dwell in abundance, rest, and safety (Deut 12:10). The promised land will also be "a dwelling for his Name" (Deut 12:11), and where harmonious relationship with God will once again reign.

You Will Be a Blessing

Willem VanGemeren adds a fourth to Clines' list of three promises: all people's on earth will be blessed through Abraham (Gen 12:3),[18] which is repeated four other times in Genesis (18:18; 22:18; 26:4; 28:14).[19] Others

---

17. Westermann, *Genesis 1–11*, 140.
18. VanGemeren, *The Progress of Redemption*, 104.
19. I am not going into the debates whether the nations will be blessed (passive, Gen 12:3; 18:18; 29:14) or will bless themselves (reflexive, Gen 22:18; 26:4), although in consideration of the consistency of the manner through which the world is saved through Jesus Christ, I lean more toward the former. For further readings on the nuances, see Lee, "Once Again," 279–96.

will also be cursed on his account. This is portrayed quite vividly in the Genesis narratives. Lot was blessed because of Abraham (Gen 12:6) and Laban admitted to be blessed due to Jacob (Gen 30:27). Abimelech, Potiphar, Pharaoh, and the Egyptians also received either blessings or punishment on account of Abraham and his descendants. This is true even today, particularly in relation to Abraham's prime descendant, Jesus Christ. People's attitude and response to the Messiah determine their destiny.

God's uttered blessings contain expectations. God blessed Adam and Eve by saying, "Be fruitful and increase in number and fill the water in the seas, and let the birds increase on the earth" (Gen 1:22). The fourth blessing to Abraham contains a responsibility placed upon him and his descendants. This will be discussed more fully in the next chapter, but suffice it to say here that God's salvific operation in the world requires servants. God chose the one nation of Israel for the sake of the many nations. Through their abundant and holy lives, people of surrounding nations will know who God is (2 Kgs 19:19; Isa 37:20; Ezek 39:7). The Israelites are supposedly God's suffering servants for the nations (Isa 41:8; 42:19; 43:10; 44:1–2, 21; 45:5; 48:20; 49:3). Of course, the quintessential seed ultimately refers and finds it consummation in Jesus Christ (see Matt 1:1–17). The prophesied Suffering Servant is an individual (Isa 49:5–7; 50:10; 52:13; 53:11) who would experience being wounded for our healing (Isa 53:5; cf. Gen 3:21). The parallel between Adam and Jesus Christ in Romans 5:12–21 also illustrates that if sin and death came to the world through one man, salvation and life also comes through the one mediator (1 Tim 2:5). He is the ultimate One for the many: "The Son of Man did not come to be served, but to serve, and to give his life as a ransom for many" (Mark 10:45). The world—with all its nations—is blessed and saved through him (John 3:16–17).

Conclusions

The universal story that God inaugurated in creation continued in the calling of Abraham to be blessed and be a blessing. Like the act of creating time and space and everything in it, God took the initiative in inviting and gathering people to himself in relationship. Sin and death are not the final words. In his freedom and grace, God reaches out to humanity and opens himself to "the different other." His covenant with Noah not to destroy the world is complimented by his act of blessing it. Abraham represents the new beginning of God's work. God's *modus operandi* is to choose one person through whom many others may be blessed. Abraham was chosen for the sake of all. Through him and his descendants, particularly Jesus Christ, all nations will be blessed. Of course, between the calling of Abraham and the birth of Jesus Christ is the long history of the people of Israel. The covenant that God established with them, his mighty works of deliverance, and his act in transforming them into a holy priesthood are all within God's work of redemption. It is about this in-between time that we shall turn to in the next chapter. Through the history of Israel, we will see other superimposing aspects of God's saving grace.

4

Relational Grace

> "Out of all nations you will be my treasured possession. Although the whole earth is mine, you will be for me a kingdom of priests and a holy nation"
>
> —EXODUS 19:5–6

IT IS IMPORTANT TO understand God's saving work by looking at the witness of the whole Scripture. The universal drama of salvation begins with the fact that "God saw everything that he has made . . . it was very good" (Gen 1:31), followed by an antithetical "God saw the earth, and it was corrupt" (Gen 6:12). Out of fear and shame, self-centeredness, and self-preservation, we humans rely on our own ingenuity to solve the problems we have brought upon ourselves. But only God can save us. In his generous mercy, he reaches out to invite us to his communion of love. When he saved Noah and called Abraham, God was acting for the sake of the world. Though Noah, humanity can continue to exist; through Abraham, nations will be blessed. The universal blessing through Abraham's descendants, however, did not come immediately. Salvation history took a lot of unexpected detours.

Relational Grace

Grace of Deliverance

Ironically, when God fulfilled his promise in giving Abraham numerous offspring (Exod 1:6-7), this caused fear from others, not blessedness (Exod 1:10). God's chosen people, who were destined to become blessing to the nations, became slaves in Egypt for four centuries (Exod 1:11; 12:40-41; Acts 7:6; Gal 3:16-17). God called Abraham to go to Canaan, but his descendants temporarily ended up in Egypt. Their pitiful circumstance was vividly described in Exodus 1:13-14: "[The Egyptians] made their lives bitter with harsh labor in brick and mortar and with all kinds of work in the fields; in all their harsh labor the Egyptians worked them ruthlessly." Worse still, Pharaoh ordered Israelite infanticide (Exod 1:15-16, 22). It is in the midst of this chaos and death that we learn important lessons about God's saving work. Once again, he appointed one human for the sake of the many. Moses is called to carry out God's purposes. In initiating to save them, God remembers his promises to Abraham (Exod 2:23-24). This is crucial. As in the calling of Abraham, God delivers them out of sheer grace and unconditional love. Moses spells this richly later: "The Lord did not set his affection on you and choose you because you were more numerous than other peoples, for you were the fewest of all peoples. But it was because the Lord loved you and kept the oath he swore to your ancestors that he brought you out with a mighty hand and redeemed you from the land of slavery, from the power of Pharaoh king of Egypt" (Deut 7:7-8).

Salvation and Judgment

The deliverance story from Egypt is characterized by violence, suffering, and death. Egypt experienced a series of plagues that destroyed natural resources and took human life (Exod 7:14—11:10). Instead of thinking of the Egyptians as collateral damage, there is actually a profound theological theme in the plagues. The Exodus story is a continuation of God's universal action in Genesis. Pharaoh's policies incurred God's chastisement because his sins violated the integrity and purpose of creation. Institutionalized slavery is the epitome of distorted relationships. God acted on behalf of the oppressed. The plagues are signs of creation going berserk in response to human abuse of power. In redemption, God deals with the oppressed and the oppressors alike. He saves pitiful victims and punishes evil doers. This is foreshadowed in as early as Genesis 3:15, when God spoke of the serpent's head being crushed (see Rom 16:20). Judgment of evil and wrongdoing accompanies the salvation of God's people (Ps 97:2–3).

We see this theme throughout Scriptures. "Those who oppose the Lord," Hannah proclaimed, "will be broken ... the Lord will judge the ends of the earth" (1 Sam 2:10). Kings and rulers may oppose God and hold temporary authority (Ps 2:2), but God "will crush all those kingdoms and bring them to an end" (Dan 2:44; Ezek 25–33; Joel 3:1–8; Zech 9–14). Even the saving work of Jesus Christ entails the defeat and judgment of evil. Jesus is portrayed as a rider on a horse who throws the beast and his minions into a fiery lake (Rev 19:11–16, 19–21). They are brought to punishment. Gustaf Aulén sees this as a dominant view in the early church in interpreting the saving work of Christ.[1] The clearest biblical support is Hebrews 2:14–15: Jesus shared in our humanity so that "by his death he might break the power of him who holds the power of death—that is, the devil—and free those who all their lives were held in slavery by their fear of death." For humans to experience true liberation, the enemy needs to be dealt with decisively on our behalf. The destruction of Egypt foreshadows the fall of all forms of powers and authorities that attempt to thwart God's purposes for his creation. Because of Pharaoh's stubbornness, the last of the ten plagues killed the firstborn of Egyptian households, slaves, and cattle (Exod 11:5; 12:12). This is the just wage of sin.

Salvation and Blood

While the torrent of death ravaged the oppressors in Egypt, divine movement of grace enveloped the Israelites. He came to save them through Moses, and he would accomplish his purposes even when the Israelites were still in Egypt. God saved the Israelites by commanding them to kill a lamb and "take some of the blood and put it on the sides and tops of the doorframes of their houses" (Exod 12:7). Their obedience is the "material gesture" of their confidence in God's protection.[2] The blood does not hide the Israelites from God's eyes; rather, it reveals them as God's possessions. He would spare them from death when he sees it. Blood was the visible sign of God's promise of life. It must be highlighted that God's visitation on the night of the tenth plague is not geographically limited. God visits every home in Egypt, including the Israelites' in Goshen. Everyone equally stands

---

1. Aulén, *Christus Victor*.
2. Brueggemann, *Reverberations of Faith*, 183.

before the judgment seat of God. God's object of punishment is Egyptian oppression and idolatry, not its mere citizens. The Israelites, therefore, are implicated. Having been in Egypt for four centuries, the Israelites have already assimilated Egyptian lifestyle and worship. Their constant rebellion in the wilderness and tendency to return to their Egyptian ways are evidence of this. Salvation from death is not ethnically determined. They are spared only because they listened to and obeyed God's instruction. They are not saved because of the blood of Abraham flowing through their veins; they are saved only through the blood of the lamb. Of course, the first Passover prefigures most of the temple's sacrificial system (temple sacrificial system did not always require blood sacrifice for the forgiveness of sin; see Num 5:11–13) and the salvific work of Jesus Christ. Redemption is ultimately through Jesus' blood (Eph 1:7; Rom 3:25).

Salvation From and To

In delivering the Israelites from Egypt, God reveals his gracious redemptive purposes for all humanity and provides us with a glimpse how he would save us. The consequence of sin is banishment and scattering (Gen 2:22–24; 11:8), but the consequence of God's grace is gathering back to his presence. It is the restoration of worship and community.[3] The Israelites were called out of oppression and scarcity into living in a land of blessing. Salvation is not merely deliverance from an unfavorable state of affairs; it is also initiation to a life of peace, abundance, dignity, and service. Leaving Egypt is not complete without meeting God at Mt. Sinai and entering Canaan.

Deliverance from slavery is quite symbolic. God intended humanity to live in equality and mutual support. Being dominated by another entails life in peril. Selfish rule leads to exploitation, poverty, and ultimately, death. Humans with corrupted political image treat other persons as non-persons. They live in sin, which is characterized by refusal to love, rejection of fellowship, and using others at their expense. This was the Egyptian predicament. From this inhumane situation, God delivers Israel for a life of peace, well-being, security, equality, and fellowship. God leads them toward Mt. Sinai to receive laws that promote social cohesion and harmony. In the words of Terence E. Fretheim, "the Decalogue provides an apodictic [absolute truth] form of 'core values' . . . These values are concerned most fundamentally with promoting and protecting the life and well-being of the *community*,

---

3. Fretheim, *The Pentateuch*, 110.

indeed the good order of creation."[4] The laws might appear stringent, but God's intention is for them to exist in love (Rom 13:8–10).

God's Chosen People

The focal point of the entire Exodus narrative is Mt. Sinai. The Israelites come out of Egypt in order to meet God in worship (Exod 3:12) and be established as his covenant people. "Out of all nations you will be my treasured possession," God said, "you will be for me a kingdom of priests and a holy nation" (Exod 19:5–6). Covenant-making is God's means of reaching and inviting creation into intimate relationship. There is a close relationship between redemption and covenant. God intervenes in moments of adverse human situations to rescue us. This is why Old Testament scholar Walter Brueggemann defines salvation as "deliverance from any and every circumstance and from any negative power that prevents full, joyous, communal existence."[5] But he does not leave us to be on our own after. Instead, he binds himself to his redeemed people. Divine grace gives two things: deliverance and God's gift of himself.

Invitation to Life

The primary implication of covenant with God is life. A covenant is not a contract of equals. The relationship between God and Israel is similar to vassal treaties found in the Ancient Near East, where the covenant is between a lord and a lesser party. But God's covenant with Israel does not oppressively curtail their freedom; it actually entails their gracious inclusion to God's communal life and reign and the gift of the law to maintain social order. The Abrahamic covenant emphasized God's promise of life; the Mosaic covenant highlighted what life with God means.

As we have seen in chapter 1, God designed humans to enjoy life in abundance. In leading them to a land flowing with milk and honey (Exod 3:8, 17; 13:5; 33:3), God was inviting them to enjoy life once again. The spies sent by Moses confirmed that the land indeed had abundant livestock and plants (Num 13:27). In fact, the north of present-day Israel was once

---

4. Fretheim, *The Pentateuch*, 106–7.

5. Brueggemann, *Reverberations of Faith*, 185. This is why William D. Barrick writes that "covenants appear to have been promulgated at times of crisis of change when God's people were upon the threshold of the unknown," in "The Mosaic Covenant," 215.

part of Mesopotamia, also known as "the Fertile Crescent." Interestingly, Egypt itself was a prosperous region. Large parts of Egypt were fertile because of the river Nile, yet God preferred for the Israelites to leave and go into "a good and spacious land" (Exod 3:8). Why was this so? God's presence is crucial. Peace is not merely the absence of unfavorable situations or living in abundance; it is primarily the presence of God. This is why God's action is: "I will free you from being slaves to them . . . I will take you as my own people, and I will be your God" (Exod 6:6–7). God's indwelling is his greatest gift (Lev 26:11). Reminiscent of the Garden of Eden, he will walk among his people (Lev 26:12). His dwelling is forever (1 Kgs 6:13) and his covenant is everlasting (Gen 9:12; 15:18; 17:7, 17; Exod 2:24; Lev 26:42; Deut 29:13; 2 Kgs 12:23).

God initiated a covenant with the Israelites to be a distinct people. He gave them the Torah, "wherein Israel's life in covenantal obedience is fully explicated."[6] Although God unilaterally promulgated the stipulations of the covenant, God is not violently imposing his unreasonable will upon them. The Torah is "the way of the Lord" (Ps 119:1). In giving the law, therefore, he reveals his nature as the Holy God of love, order, and community. The commandments are also protective in nature and function, meant to preserve the nation and to maintain solidarity with God and others. Consideration of the Ten Commandments reveals God's intention for the Israelites to live in love and peace, vertically and horizontally. Six of the ten pertain to human interaction in the family and among others in the community (Exod 20:3–17; Deut 5:7–21). Interestingly, a large portion of the Holiness Code deals with interpersonal relationships (Lev 17–26). Moses aptly summarizes the purpose of the law: "The Lord commanded us to obey all these decrees and to fear the Lord our God, *so that we might always prosper and be kept alive*, as is the case today" (Deut 6:24, italics mine). The covenant is concerned with justice, mercy, equality, and love, because it is only in having these that humans could truly enjoy life.

Grace and Law

God emphasizes volitional moral responsibility. He demands radical faithfulness and obedience, which the Israelites unanimously consented and committed themselves to do (Exod 19:8; 24:3; 24:7). The order of grace is profound. Nothing was demanded from them prior to their exodus from

6. Brueggemann, *Reverberations of Faith*, 218.

Egypt. Their deliverance is entirely God's gracious initiative; they could not free themselves. The commandments were given after they were set free. This appears to be God's *modus operandi* in salvation. Abraham received promises before commanded to be circumcised. The saving work of Jesus Christ follows this principle: "while we were still sinners, Christ died for us" (Rom 5:8). The Father did not require global repentance before the Son was sent into the world. Confession and repentance are our responses to grace, not conditions for grace. The law was "never designed for the recovery of the favour and life of God once lost, but only for the continuance and increase thereof"[7] (i.e., of grace). None can establish their own righteousness through the law. Obedience to the law is not a coin-earned merit to bribe God to grant salvation. "Recovery of the favour and the life of God, requires only faith," Wesley writes. Obedience to the law, in gratitude, is for "man's continuance in the favour of God, in his knowledge and love, in holiness and happiness."[8]

Salvation and Transformation

God wanted the Israelites to conduct themselves in a manner worthy of being his own people. The Israelites, unfortunately, were not easily pliable. They were torn between their willingness and unwillingness to put Egypt— its religious and social consciousness—behind them. They were happy to leave Egypt's oppression but struggled to break free from its worldview. They found it difficult to recognize that the law is a blessing (Deut 4:8; 30:11–14; Ps 19:9–11). Being under oppression for so long, they desired little restriction. Moreover, having lived in Egypt for several generations, they have assimilated Egyptian culture. Reverting back to their familiar ways of life and worship was their default response. This is why it was easy for them to create a golden calf to worship even when they were at the foot of God's mountain (Exod 32:1–20). In giving the law, God was undoing their previous ways of thought and was creating in them a new mindset.[9]

This is where we realize the inseparability between revelation and transformation. When my wife revealed that she does not like me playing computer games, she was revealing something about herself. But her self-revelation also meant that I have to change if I were to stay in relationship

---

7. Wesley, "Righteousness of Faith," *Works* (BE) 1: 210.
8. Wesley, "Righteousness of Faith," *Works* (BE) 1: 209.
9. Letham, "'Not a Covenant of Works,'" 147–49.

with her. The objective of revelation is not information, but transformation. This generated a conflictive relationship between God and Israel. In the words of Thomas F. Torrance,

> The more deeply the Word of God penetrated into the innermost depths of Israel's existence and embodied itself within, the more it seemed to burn like fire in its bones until the prophets who were burdened with the Word of the Lord cried out in agony. To be the bearer of divine revelation is to suffer, and not only to suffer but to be killed and made alive again, and not only to be made alive but to be continually renewed and refashioned under its impact.[10]

The covenant between God and Israel was not a covenant between God and righteous people. Rather, it was between the Holy God and rebellious, stubborn, stiff-necked Israel (Exod 32:9; Ps 78:8, 40). The more God drew himself closer to Israel in revelation and grace, the more the Israelites opposed him. God challenged the basic structure of Israel's ways of life, but they were unwilling to be re-shaped. Instead of condemning the Israelites, however, Torrance says the conflict between Israel and God mirrors the conflict between God and ourselves. Being holy, just as God is holy, entails our absolute compliance with God's will. There is a habituated resistance of the human soul, acclimated to the ways of the world, to the transforming will of God. Ironically, the degree of human rebellion is often proportionate to the level of divine magnanimity.

A Holy Worshipping Nation

Israel's identity as God's chosen is very specific. It is a holy nation. The Israelites are set apart for worship. "Restoration of true worship," N. T. Wright asserts, is "the goal of the covenant."[11] They are to recognize and worship the only one true God. "I am the Lord," Yahweh proclaimed, "and there is no other; apart from me there is no God" (Isa 45:5). The law begins with this affirmation. Freedom of religious choice was not conceded. Other religions in the land are ruthlessly dealt with, particularly by the prophets. The allegiance and service of Israel should belong solely to Yahweh. Idolatry is the anti-thesis of holiness. Monotheism is a national holiness statement. Wright sees this theme even in the New Testament. He writes, dealing

---

10. Torrance, *The Mediation of Christ*, 10–11.
11. Wright, *The Day the Revolution Began*, 316.

Grace and Salvation

particularly with Romans 2:17—4:25, that it "is all about God's covenant with Israel and through Israel for the world and about the true worship as the heart of his covenant, the worship of the one true God, which replaces the idolatry of 1:18–23 and thus undoes the sin of 1:24–32."[12] God's covenant-making mission ends in worship.

Worship, however, is not an intermittent event in the life of God's people. It is a *lifestyle*. This is reflected in the Hebrew *ebed* or *avad* (Exod 3:12; Ps 100:2; Deut 10:12–13) and Greek *latreuo* (Acts 24:14; Rom 12:1), both meaning "to serve" or "service." To worship is to serve and to serve is to worship. We worship God every moment of every day and wherever we are. Worship is the conscious and uninterrupted offering of our bodies to God (Rom 12:1). It is a life of integrity and consistency, and hence it has moral-ethical connotations (Rom 6:13). As C. E. B. Cranfield asserted, this implies that "the true worship which God desires embraces the whole of the Christian's life from day to day. It implies that any cultic worship which is not accompanied by obedience in the ordinary affairs of life must be regarded as false worship, unacceptable to God."[13] Worship is not an abrupt supernatural event in a life characterized generally by an "ever-increasing wickedness" (Rom 6:20), as if worship is a miraculous interposition of something sacred amid our ungodly routine. This is why worship is closely connected with the "fear of the Lord," because to fear God "is to obey his voice" (1 Sam 12:14), to walk in his ways (Deut 8:6), to keep his commandments (Ecc 12:13), and to turn away from evil (Job 1:1; Prov 3:7).[14] True worship is characterized by obedience and service to God.

Others might look for technological advancement, environmental equilibrium, or pursuit of knowledge as the hallmark of their societies. Not so with the people of God. Holiness is the goal of God's people. The challenge, however, is in expecting holiness from an entire nation, not only from a few extraordinary persons. No Israelite is exempted from obeying the law. As a nation, they are to reflect the character of God in every aspect of their lives. This is why the law encompasses religious, political, social, familial, interpersonal, and even hygienic aspects of everyday existence. God's holiness must be seen not only in the temple; it must be lived out at home, in the marketplace, in the streets, and in the king's

---

12. Wright, *The Day the Revolution Began*, 315.

13. Cranfield, *A Critical and Exegetical Commentary on the Epistle to the Romans*, 601.

14. See Webber, *Worship Old and New*, 29–30.

palace. Holiness must be reflected in people's relationship with God and in their treatment of others.

The Israelites were to be different from others. They should not be swallowed by the prevailing cultures of foreign countries. "You must not do as they do in Egypt, where you used to live, and you must not do as they do in the land of Canaan, where I am bringing you. Do not follow their practices," God said. They "must obey his laws and be careful to follow his decrees" (Lev 18:3–4; Ezek 20:19). Because Israel is God's "treasured possession," the nation should live according to his character as their sovereign benefactor. Through the law, God revealed his holy nature and intention to create a people like himself; hence the command, "Be holy for I am holy" (Lev 11:44–45; 19:2; 20:7). The Israelites struggled to live up to God's expectations. The transformation that God's presence demanded happened very slowly and with plenty of resistance. They are *positionally* holy by virtue of their relationship with God but the *moral* outworking of their holy identity was progressive. Ultimately, it is God's faithfulness that makes them holy, not their own performance. Wright explains why their holy identity is not stripped from them amidst their failures: "God's faithfulness to the covenant with Israel . . . will result in the rescue of the whole sinful world."[15] This is an important point, particularly because their vocation to the whole world is inseparable from their identity.

A Kingdom of Priests

The holy nation is also "a kingdom of priests" (Exod 19:6). This has political connotations. Kingdoms are not typically governed by or primarily composed of priests. Royal priesthood is both a statement of national identity and missional calling. Israel represents Yahweh to the world. Another holiness dimension is separation for God's use. Ceremonial holiness, emphasized by temple priests, refers to the holiness of things as they are set apart for exclusive temple use. Worship accessories, utensils, and other implements are holy things because they belong to God *and* are used by him and for him. As priests, the Israelites belong to God and are his agents in the world. This is their holiness as a worshipping people. God's blessing to the world will flow through them. They must usher people into God's presence and mediate between God and humanity. This is their worship—their service—to God.

15. Wright, *The Day the Revolution Began*, 316.

Grace and Salvation

The Israelites are priests passively and actively. Through God's act of delivering the Israelites from a powerful nation such as Egypt, nations will know who God is and fear him. God himself said, "But this is why I have let you live: to show you my power, and to make my name resound through all the earth" (Exod 9:16). Israelite leaders recognized this.

> "For the Lord your God dried up the Jordan . . . so that all the peoples of the earth might know that the hand of the Lord is powerful" (Josh 4:23-24)

> "You performed signs and wonders against Pharaoh and all his servants and all the people of his land . . . You made a name for yourself, which remains to this day" (Neh 9:10)

This aspect of priesthood is passive. God is the primary actor. But the divine favors they received have missional implications. Hezekiah prayed for deliverance from the Assyrian army "so that all the kingdoms of the earth may know that you, LORD, are God alone" (2 Kgs 19:19; Isa 37:20). Ezekiel prophesied about God's restoration of Israel after exile, not for Israel's sake, but so that "the nations may know that he is the LORD" (36:22-23; cf. 36:38; 38:23; 39:7). The Israelites realized that if others experience the same favor they received from God, God is also revealed. This is why Solomon asked God to answer the foreigner's prayer "so that all the peoples of the earth may know your name and fear you, as do your people Israel" (1 Kgs 8:41-43; 2 Chr 6:32-33). When neighboring nations talk about Israel, they will realize who Yahweh is. In the words of the psalmist:

> May God be gracious to us and bless us
> and make his face to shine upon us,
> that your way may be known upon earth,
> your saving power among all nations.
> Let the peoples praise you, O God;
> let all the peoples praise you (Ps 67:1-3, ESV)

Because God is associated with Israel, however, the opposite can also happen. Whatever they do will be known by all nations, which can bring either honor to Yahweh or defile his name. God wanted Israel to live holy lives so that his name would be known as the holy God throughout the whole earth (Exod 9:16; Ps 106:8; 2 Sam 7:23; 2 Kgs 19:19; Isa 37:20; Ezek 36:22-23; 36:38; 38:23; 39:7; Ps 67:1-3). His complaint is that they were accomplishing the opposite. Yahweh laments that "wherever they went among the nations they profaned my holy name . . . I had concern for my holy name, which the people of Israel profaned among the nations where they had gone" (Ezek 36:20–21; see also Exod 20:7; Lev 18:21; 19:12; 20:1–5; 22:32; Prov 30:9; Isa 52:5–6; Jer 34:16; Ezek 13:19; 20:9, 14, 22, 27, 39; 22:16; 29:14; 36:20; Amos 2:7; Mal 1:12). The frequency Yahweh expressed this reveals the heartening failure of Israel.

Of course, passivity was not only what God had in mind for the Israelites. The word "kingdom" in the "kingdom of priests" strongly denotes activism and intentional missions. There is logic in this. When people see our blessed lives, they are not automatically led to God. At best, people become curious, but ultimately, they may be saved when someone tells them the gospel. This seems to be what Paul had in mind when he wrote Romans 10:14–15: "How, then, can they call on the one they have not believed in? And how can they believe in the one of whom they have not heard? And how can they hear without someone preaching to them? And how can anyone preach unless they are sent?" Lifestyle evangelism must be accompanied by public worship and proclamation.

In the whole drama of salvation, the designation of Israel as a "kingdom of priests" also entails the restoration of humanity to its proper calling and vocation. When God commanded the representative humans to "rule over" creatures, the Hebrew word used is *radah,* a term used for royalty (Gen 1:28). Kings in the Ancient Near East were considered god's representatives on earth. They are privileged as chosen ones, but they also bear the responsibility of being the arms and feet of gods. Humans are created to function "in place of the gods, in service of the gods, and on behalf of the gods."[16] When God appointed humanity as *radah,* he was delegating them to perform his work in the cosmos as royal priests. So when God called Israel as a kingdom of priests, he was redeeming and reinstating humanity to their royal status as his stewards. Blessings will flow to the nations through the labor of their hands. The whole earth is God's temple and the Israelites are the appointed priests. Through the one nation God chose, all nations will receive divine favor. As Fretheim expresses:

> "Priestly" has reference to being mediators between God and the nations not unlike a priest functions in a religious community; holy has a reference to a people set apart, not simply *from* other peoples, but *for* a specific purpose. Together, then, the phrases refer to Israel's vocation to be God's people among the nations. The phrases look not inward, but outward beyond the self or the

---

16. Walton, *The Lost World of Adam and Eve,* 90; Davies, *A Royal Priesthood,* 85, 152.

community. This is also the interpretation given by 1 Pet 2:9, which also picks up on Exodus 9:16 (and, implicitly, 15:1–21) in its concern for proclaiming the works of God.[17]

Walking with God

The identity and mission of the Israelites were set in place at Mt. Sinai. Their journey as a nation, however, was just starting. They just received the law. They were not automatically transformed by it. The long wandering between Goshen and the promised land is characterized by fear, not faith. The Israelites complained and murmured against Moses even prior to their arrival at Mt. Sinai (Exod 15:24; 16:2–3). They felt victims of injustice, preferring their circumstances in Egypt as slaves over their freed conditions in the desert (Exod 14:12; Num 14:3). The psalmist sums it up well: "Our fathers in Egypt did not grasp Your wonders or remember Your abundant kindness; but they rebelled by the sea" (Ps 106:7, BSB). In the face of difficulties, their default response was to retreat and murmur. They struggled with the idea of servitude to God. They resented standards and feared responsibilities. The conflict, Michael Walzer asserts, was between "the materialism of the people and the idealism of their leaders" or between "the demands of the present moment and the promise of the future."[18]

After staying at Sinai Peninsula for almost a year, the Israelites headed north. They stopped at Kadesh Barnea and sent spies (Num 13:1–33). For their unbelief, their next 38 years were characterized by further rebellion and death. But amidst their tragedies, we realize something profound about God. He remains faithful to and patient with his own people. Disaster is always interrupted by acts of divine grace. This had been how God acted since Genesis, but the magnitude of his graciousness is amplified in his dealings with the Israelites. He intervenes in their lack of food (Exod 16:1–15), provides them water (Exod 17:1–7), cures them of fatal diseases (Num 21:6–9), defeats their enemies (Exod 17:8–13), and relents from exterminating them (Exod 32:11–14). God responded graciously to every crisis they met.[19] He saved them all throughout their journey. Something profound is happening

17. Fretheim, *The Pentateuch*, 116.
18. Walzer, *Exodus and Revolution*, 51.
19. J. Coert Rylaarsdam notes that throughout the history of salvation, this is how God acts: "The saving act of Yahweh was completely adequate and utterly decisive to meet the crisis that was its occasion," in "Jewish-Christian Relationships," 74.

in the story. Fretheim concludes that the exodus story—from Egypt to Canaan—is God's continuing creation and re-creation that started in Genesis. In short, God was not only saving humans; he was also redeeming the whole earth. Fretheim writes:

> The created order was adversely affected by Egyptian anticreational policies. But now, on the far side of cosmic victory, the wilderness springs into new life. The water that could not be drunk in the first plague is now made potable (7:24; 15:23, 27; 17:5–6); the heavens that "rained" hail, destroying food sources, now "rain" bread (9:18, 23; 16:4); instead of the locusts that "come up" and "cover" the ground, destroying plant life (10:14–15), the quails "come up" and "cover" the ground, providing food (16:13).[20]

The wilderness experience is Israel's forward march toward several goals. More important than physical entrance to the promised land was their journey towards communal transformation. The desert was the cauldron where the remnants of Egyptian mindset are purged and replaced by Yahweh's divine will. As indicated above, the transforming experience was not seamless. In a sense, the Israelites blazed the trail even for Christians today. They showed what it means to experience the process of transformation, along with the challenges and oppositions that come from hearts where old mindset and habits are deeply entrenched. Pseudo-Macarius in the fourth century argued that even among Christians, transformation and growth are slow. The battle between the old self we need to leave behind and the new self we need to become is painfully real. Of course, the Israelite wilderness experience does not represent the ideal Christian life. Although young believers may have ups and downs, this need not be the case for life. Through the enabling and empowering Holy Spirit, there must come a point in our lives when we are victorious over our selfishness and over Satan's temptations. Nevertheless, there is merit in considering the Israelite experience. Pastorally, we need to be aware that sin is so ingrained in humanity that the process of transformation may be slow for some. This is probably why David used *kabac* when he asked God to wash away his sins (Ps 51:1–2). The word describes washing clothes by beating them with a paddle or rock in the river. Sin is so entrenched in the human heart like a stain that it literally needs to be beaten out of us. Cleansing and purification from sin are slow and painful experiences.

---

20. Fretheim, *The Pentateuch*, 119.

Grace and Salvation

Promised Land

The exodus story has a beginning, middle, and end. These three parts are characterized by a problem (Egypt), a struggle (wilderness), and a resolution (promised land). The land symbolizes productivity (Joel 3:18; Amos 9:13; Zech 1:17), healing and restoration (Jer 33:6–8; Jer 30:18; Isa 61:4; Ezek 36:10; Mic 4:8), and protection from enemies (Isa 62:8–9; Joel 3:16).[21] "The story of Israel and its land," Wright argues "is set in deliberate parallel to the story of Adam and Eve in the garden."[22] Thus, entrance to the promised land can be seen as the return of humanity to a second Garden of Eden. First, like the Garden, Canaan has abundant food. It is where large grapes grow, along with figs and pomegranates (Num 13:23). Second, like in the Garden, God will dwell with the Israelites in Canaan (Exod 33:14; Josh 1:9). Third, like in the Garden where there was unbroken human relationship between Adam and Eve, they are going to live in Canaan in equality and prosperity, in accordance with God's covenant laws. The promised land is a place of life.[23]

Conclusions

God's salvific work is both personal and communal. He saves an entire nation out of sheer grace. Through those he saved, others might also receive blessings. He calls people from their deathly predicament, gathers them unto himself in intimate relationship, transforms them into his own image, and anoints them to be his worshipping servants. From the exodus story, we realize several things about God's saving methods. First, it is by grace that we are saved (Eph 2:8–9). The Israelites were saved not because of their merits, but because God seeks to create a people who will faithfully make him known to the nations. In all circumstances God remains faithful to himself and to his promises (Deut 7:7–8). Second, salvation entails deliverance from oppressive and usurping powers. Freedom from all forms of bondage—physical, social, and spiritual—is the shape of redemption (John 8:36; Gal 5:1; 2 Cor 3:17). Third, God punishes the wicked and brings them to shame (Col 2:15). Fourth, salvation also has anticipatory elements. We

---

21. Vasholz, "The Character of Israel's Future in Light of the Abrahamic and Mosaic Covenants," 46.

22. Wright, *The Day the Revolution Began*, 94–96.

23. Soller, "A Latch and Clasp," 14.

are saved from our predicament and are invited to communion with God and enjoy his blessings. Fifth, those who are called by God are also "transformed into his image with ever-increasing glory" (2 Cor 3:18). Sixth, it is by living the holy life that we can fulfill our mission to be blessings to the nations. This is our responsibility as God's chosen people. Finally, salvation is a dynamic and ongoing experience. Having been already saved, we have to remain in God and be careful to keep his laws. Our relationship with God is ever-growing.

The covenant is an ongoing dialogue between God's revelation and human response. God does not operate by divine fiat, micro-managing every aspect of Israelite life. Rather, he makes his redeemed people responsible to the grace they received. Unfortunately, having already received the promise, the Israelites started to feel comfortable. Because of their disobedience, they suffered defeats—military and religious—from without and within. Like Adam and Eve, they failed to obey God's decrees that were meant to guide them towards enjoying the gifts of relationship and life. After settling in the land, they lived in their idolatrous inclinations. Nehemiah narrates their tragic story:

> Their children went in and took possession of the land. You subdued before them the Canaanites, who lived in the land; you gave the Canaanites into their hands, along with their kings and the peoples of the land, to deal with them as they pleased. They captured fortified cities and fertile land; they took possession of houses filled with all kinds of good things, wells already dug, vineyards, olive groves and fruit trees in abundance. They ate to the full and were well-nourished; they reveled in your great goodness. But they were disobedient and rebelled against you; they turned their backs on your law. They killed your prophets, who had warned them in order to turn them back to you; they committed awful blasphemies (Neh 9:24–26).

The Israelites easily forgot the stipulations of the covenant. They were called to be holy. He demanded faith in him alone. The Israelites misunderstood their privileged identity. They neglected that "the Abrahamic Covenant is unconditionally and everlastingly guaranteed to the seed of Abraham, but enjoyment of those promised blessings was conditioned on obedience."[24] A new oppression swept over them as a consequence of their disobedience (Judg 3:7, 12; 4:1). Even the saved can fall from grace.

---

24. Townsend, "Fulfillment of the Land Promise in the Old Testament," 331.

5

Restoration and Renewal

"I will take you out of the nations; I will gather you from all the countries and bring you back into your own land. I will sprinkle clean water on you, and you will be clean; I will cleanse you from all your impurities and from all your idols. I will give you a new heart and put a new spirit in you; I will remove from you your heart of stone and give you a heart of flesh"

—EZEKIEL 36:24–26

THE DYNAMIC RELATIONSHIP BETWEEN God's initiative and human accountability leaves us with a deep sense of appreciation of God's gift of freedom and a sincere angst about the consequences of its misuse. It is mysterious how God's gracious works—in giving life, establishing covenants, and fulfilling promises—are easily interrupted by human ingratitude. This is portrayed in the lives of the Israelites. After having been miraculously delivered from Egypt, and amidst their repeated rebellion, they finally entered the promised land through Joshua's leadership. Although the temple stood as a symbol of the centrality of worship and holiness and ritual-festivals were celebrated to commemorate Yahweh's mighty acts, corruption spread throughout the land, particularly through the kings. The consequence of their disobedience was the exile. Yet in the bleakness of their deposition, God's faithful love springs to action and saves them once more. The exile,

Rainer Albertz writes, should not only be perceived "as a terrible catastrophe but also as a God-given chance for a new beginning."[1] Several important themes concerning grace and salvation are found in this segment of salvation history.

Political and Theological Exile

Politically, the exile serves as evidence of Babylonian expansion and theologically as the end of Yahweh's patience with his chosen people. It is the ultimate consequence of the sins of Israel as a whole, resulting in the loss of Israel's most important things: the temple, the monarchy, the land, and the city of Jerusalem. Although it is significantly shorter than their Egyptian bondage, it shattered many of Israel's conceived notions about their privileges as God's chosen people. At least, they unashamedly recognized that the exile demonstrated God's judgment (see also Acts 7:43). This was why one of Ezekiel's pastoral burdens was to explain God's action to the suffering people. For Ezekiel, "judgment is to be understood in terms of the absolute rightness of an action which has fallen upon the whole people. He is concerned to demonstrate how the disaster fits into the plan and purpose of God, and to show how the condition of the people is such that any alternative is unthinkable."[2]

The central issues were idolatry and apostasy. The kingdoms of Israel and Judah, under the leadership of many wicked kings, exchanged worship of Yahweh for other gods. Israel was led astray by the surrounding nations through intermarriages (e.g., Solomon, 1 Kgs 11:1–8). Their apostasy is evident in the establishment of worship places in Bethel and Dan (1 Kgs 12:26–32) and their worship of other gods (Judg 2:12, 17; 10:13; 1 Sam 8:8). Their forgetfulness of who God is, what he has done for them, and who they are as his chosen people lie at the very root of their sin.[3] They also did not listen to the ominous "therefore" warnings of the prophets (Amos 3:2; Mic 3:9–12). Because of this, Jeremiah proclaimed God to be against Judah (Jer 1:4–10, 15–16). Their destruction through Nebuchadnezzar was God's decree (Lam 2:1–10; 4:11–16). "It was not blind stroke of destiny, not ultimately the military power of Babylon, but Yahweh himself who destroyed

---

1. Albertz, *Israel in Exile*, 7.
2. Ackyord, *Exile and Restoration*, 105.
3. Brueggemann, *Hopeful Imagination*, 33.

Grace and Salvation

Jerusalem, the temple and the monarchy."[4] It is Israel's disobedience that needs to be blamed. The exile is "a political and theological state rather than a geographical one."[5] As N. T. Wright argues, it persists even to the present. The rebellions against the Greeks and Romans later in the history of Israel illustrate the longing of Israel to be truly home, at home. The contemporaneity of the exile in Jewish consciousness is evident in Matthew's decision to devote significant attention to it in his historical preamble to the saving life of Jesus (Matt 1:12–13, 17).

The Babylonian invasion brought national havoc. Both those who remained and were exiled suffered. Excavations by Kathleen Kenyon revealed ruins and rubbles of destroyed buildings (Lam 2:2) and evidence of subpar human living conditions for those who stayed (Lam 5:2–5).[6] It was the poorest of the land who were left behind (Ezek 24:14; 25:12). They referred to themselves as "slaves in our land" (Neh 9:36–37), confirmed by an inscription by Nebuchadnezzar saying, "I forced them to work . . . I imposed on them the brick basket."[7] The substantial destruction and population loss contributed to the overall socio-economic instability. Those who were deported to Babylon lost their home and property (Ezek 11:15; 33:24). Their problem was not economic, because they easily integrated in Babylonian society (Jer 2:9). Their tribulations were primarily political, psychological, and religious. Politically, they lost the influence they enjoyed at home. Psychologically, they needed to grapple with their commitment to Yahweh, whom they felt already abandoned them. Religiously, they became aware of the destruction of the temple in Jerusalem and that many religious articles were brought to Babylon. They were struck by grief (Ps 137:1–4). Even though they continued to worship Yahweh, "mourning and lamentation characterized the main cult of the exile."[8] These are evident in Psalm 42, 60, 74, 79, 89, and the book of Lamentations. The laments, however, serve also as antidote to the possibility of amnesia. Thus, in self-imprecatory declarations, they sang:

---

4. Albertz, *A History of Israelite Religion in the Old Testament Period*, 378; Ackyord, *Exile and Restoration*, 43–49.

5. Wright, *Paul and the Faithfulness of God*, 139. Bryan disagrees with Wright, arguing instead that the exile has truly ended, but full restoration had not followed, in "The End of Exile," 107–26.

6. Smith-Christopher, *A Biblical Theology of Exile*, 59.

7. Smith-Christopher, *A Biblical Theology of Exile*, 67.

8. Albertz, *A History of Israelite Religion*, 377.

> If I forget you, Jerusalem, may my right hand forget its skill.
> May my tongue cling to the roof of my mouth if I do not remember you,
> if I do not consider Jerusalem my highest joy (Ps 137:5–6)

Hope and Salvation

Lament was just one of the responses of the Israelites to their abject condition. They nurtured a hope of return to the promised land. To counter complete assimilation to Babylonian culture, they established close-knit relationships based on kinship and innovated religious-ceremonial activities that replaced temple sacrifice, like synagogue worship.[9] The prophets, aside from explaining their condition as God's punishment, also spoke oracles of salvation. If the pre-exilic era was dominated by oracles of judgment and disaster, the exilic era saw the proliferation of salvation oracles.[10] The Israelites were called to rejoice for the promise of deliverance (Isa 54:1–3; Zeph 3:14–15; Zech 2:14–16). Like pastors comforting people in their darkest days, prophets proclaimed calming messages of hope for the future. If Yahweh was involved in their punishment, his hand will also be upon them in their restoration. A longing for a better future—politically and religiously—was birthed out of their suffering. The Israelite crisis, therefore, laid the foundation for several important themes of renewal and salvation in the Bible. This is worth noting, because the eschatological hopes of the Israelites serve as the immediate background in understanding the coming of Jesus Christ and his message of the kingdom.

An Alternative Reality

The exilic prophets' salvation proclamation is characterized by an "invitation of imagination."[11] Instead of wallowing in despair over present realities, the prophets summoned the people to remember God's capable work to bring newness. They counseled them not to readily accept the current definition of reality set by the Babylonians, but to envision an alternative reality set by Yahweh himself in the fullness of his creating and saving grace. Isaiah in particular appeals to Israelite memory about God's miraculous

---

9. Albertz, *Israel in Exile*, 106–9.
10. Albertz, *Israel in Exile*, 167.
11. Brueggemann, *Hopeful Imagination*, 25.

interventions in the lives of their predecessors such as Abraham (51:2–3), the barren Sarah (54:1–3), Noah (54:9–11), and David (55:3). God is the same yesterday and today. He has delivered; he will do so again. They should expect God's action in giving them a future set of circumstances characterized by singing a new song (42:10), debunking Babylonian gods (46:1–2), and eating different bread (55:1–3). Their present predicament is only temporary, because the exile means that "the new place is not home and can never be home because its realities are essentially alien and inhospitable to [their] true theological identity."[12] Their future is in God's hands, not the Babylonians'. By appealing to history and evoking a different reality, Isaiah planted hope and renewed faith in their hearts.

Resurrection Themes

Ezekiel's message of salvation is packaged differently. In a striking vision (Ezek 37:1–14), Israel is likened to a valley of dry bones. The analogy is fitting and relevant, because Jerusalem was literally littered with corpses after the city's collapse. Their hopelessness is clear: "Our bones are dried up and our hope is gone; we are cut off" (37:11). Their bleakness, however, is confronted by a divine proclamation that Yahweh himself "will open the graves, lead his people out of the graves and bring them into the land of Israel, and that in all this he will let himself be recognized."[13] There is an unambiguous allusion to a new exodus experience here. Yahweh will once again burst them out of their oppressed imprisonment, destroying Babylon in the process as well. The contrast between the complete collapse of all hope and the unconditional promise of revival is astounding. The response "O sovereign Lord, You alone know" to the question "Son of man, can these bones live?" strongly suggests admission of human powerlessness and affirmation of God's sovereign grace and power to accomplish anything. Those who have fallen may "stand up" again by God's grace (37:10). There is a stark contrast between being scattered bones and being "a vast army" (37:10). They will be restored to life: "I will restore you to health and restore your wounds" (Jer 30:17).

---

12. Brueggemann, *Hopeful Imagination*, 110.
13. Zimmerli, *A Commentary on the Book of the Prophet Ezekiel Chapters 25–38*, 263.

Restoration and Renewal

Homecoming

Ezekiel's message of renewal addressed the Israelites' desire for repatriation to Palestine. They will be led by God himself and will settle in their land once more (37:12–14). "God who was prepared to abandon in hostility is the God who embraces in passion. As God comes full circle, this beloved people comes full circle from terminal illness to powerful healing. Or, read historically, this people abandoned to exile is now the target of luxuriant homecoming."[14] The metaphors of Isaiah's salvation messages support this: great procession (40:1–11), gathering (43:5–6), watchmen (52:7–10), rebuilt city (44:28; 54:11–12), and celebration (42:10–17). However, the problem was not merely their deposition, but the construed absence of God which they caused (Ezek 10:18–22). They exiled God from their land and lives! (Ezek 8:6). Return to the promised land must include the return of God. This is the hopeful message of Jeremiah 30:12–17.

Newness and Wholeness

The repeated instances of God's promises of return are necessary assurances to people who are psychologically conflicted about a God who could ruthlessly drive them out of the land he promised them to settle. If the exile was God's punishment for their sins, how can they possibly make reparations that would make him undo his judgment? "How can the holy one possibly forgive again his sinful people whom he has had to drive away on account of his holiness?"[15] In response to these doubts, Yahweh makes his intention very clear: "I will take you out of the nations; I will gather you from all the countries and bring you back into your own land" (Ezek 36:24). But this is just the beginning of God's restoring work. Jeremiah 31 and Ezekiel 36 expand the Israelites' limited socio-political and economic understanding of salvation.

God's response to the exile reveals several new dimensions of his saving grace. His relationship with Israel as his chosen people remains, as evidence of his faithfulness, but God begins to talk about a "new covenant" (Jer 31:31–33; Ezek 16:60, 62; 37:26) and an "everlasting covenant" (Ezek 16:60; 37:26; Isa 55:3). This does not entail the invalidation of his previous covenants with Israel, but their intensification. There are three stages of

---

14. Brueggemann, *Hopeful Imagination*, 40.
15. Zimmerli, *Ezekiel Chapters 25–38*, 247.

renewal in Ezekiel 36, and these may also be enumerated as the very content of the new covenant. First, people of the new covenant will be purified from their sins. God would forget their apostasy and give them a fresh start (Jer 31:34). The analogy of "sprinkling" (36:25) brings to mind atonement by blood which brings forgiveness of sins (Exod 24:6; Lev 1:5, 11). Before the people can begin a new life, old adages need to be removed. Running the race of faith requires getting rid of everything that hinders and entangles (Heb 12:1). For the Israelites, these referred to idols. The covenant—old and new—must be characterized by entire devotion to God (Exod 20:2–5). God's work is comprehensive: "They will no longer defile themselves with their idols and vile images or with any of their offenses, for I will save them from all their sinful backsliding, and I will cleanse them. They will be my people, and I will be their God" (Ezek 37:23).

Second, God would give his people new heart and spirit (Ezek 36:26). This is the prospective element of salvation. Inner transformation must accompany cleansing. Forgiveness of sins deals with the past while being made new allows godly living in the present and the future. This corresponds with Jeremiah 31:33–34: "I will put my law in their minds and write it on their hearts." The law will no longer remain externally written on stone tablets but will be inscribed in their hearts. Immediate instead of mediated knowledge of God makes obedience more feasible. Moses already spoke about this: "Now what I am commanding you today is not too difficult for you or beyond your reach. It is not up in heaven, so that you have to ask, 'Who will ascend into heaven to get it and proclaim it to us so we may obey it?' Nor is it beyond the sea, so that you have to ask, 'Who will cross the sea to get it and proclaim it to us so we may obey it?' No, the word is very near you; it is in your mouth and in your heart so you may obey it" (Deut 30:11–14).

Third, and closely related to the second, God would put his spirit in the human heart (Ezek 36:27). The consequence is enabled obedience to God's decrees. God does not only cleanse his people from sin and transform them from within; he also empowers. The new self is given new strength. Inner transformation does not awaken human innate capability so that we can begin to function independently. Obedience is impossible apart from God's direct and continuous participation in our lives. God's Spirit is deposited in the hearts of people to enable what Lodahl calls "partnership in covenant."[16]

---

16. Lodahl, *The Story of God*, 119.

Sanctification of God's Name

Brueggemann asserts that God's ultimate concern in his renewing action is his holiness, majesty, and honor.[17] Although the exile placed the Israelites in a position of suffering, it is God himself who is the first and primary victim. He complains, repeatedly, that his name is profaned by the Israelites (Ezek 20:9, 14, 22, 39; 36:20, 21, 22, 23; 39:7). He has withheld his wrath for the sake of his holy name (Exod 32:11–14; Ezek 20:8–9, 13–14, 21–22), but the obstinacy of the Israelites needed to be ultimately addressed. There is no win-win situation for God. Whether it is the past and active shameful conduct of his people in idolatry (Ezek 20:39; Lev 18:21; 19:12; 20:3; 21:6; 22:2, 32) or the present and passive disgraceful condition of the people in exile (Ezek 36:20–21), God's name is defiled in the eyes of the nations. God suffers with the Israelites. He is not a sadist God gloating over the righteous predicament of his broken people. He joins the Israelites in solidarity. This is an important precursor to the crucified God later in the person and work of Jesus Christ.

God is grieved that his name has become an object of ridicule in the nations through the very people he called to reflect his holiness. God is transcendent; he cannot be mocked forever. The redemption of the Israelites, therefore, is intertwined with the redemption of his name. As Zimmerli noted, the concern is "the majesty of Yahweh and the revelation of his honor and glory. For the sake of this revelation he will not abandon his people, but will again validate his honor in the eyes of the world."[18] Yahweh proclaimed: "It is not for your sake, people of Israel, that I am going to do these things, but for the sake of my holy name, which you have profaned among the nations where you have gone. I will show the holiness of my great name, which has been profaned among the nations, the name you have profaned among them. Then the nations will know that I am the Lord, when I am proved holy through you before their eyes (Ezek 36:22–23).

Two important considerations surface here. First, it is God who sanctifies his own name by showing his benevolence and saving power to the nations. If the condition of Israel in exile dishonors him, his name will be sanctified by their redemption. Both the redeemed and the redeemer are sanctified. But God's holiness is revealed not only in his saving grace but

---

17. Brueggemann, *Hopeful Imagination*, 69–87.
18. Zimmerli, *Ezekiel Chapters 25–38*, 248; Wong, "Profanation/Sanctification," 201–39.

also in his destructive power. Ezekiel's mention of the destruction of Sidon (28:20–26) and Gog (38–39) affirms this. God's holiness is displayed in punishing sin and saving his people. Second, there is human responsibility entailed in the sanctification of God's name. Humans can profane it, as the history of Israel illustrates, but their obedience and submission to God's holy decrees can sanctify it too. The prayer that Jesus taught his disciples reveals this: "Our Father in heaven, hallowed be your name" (Matt 6:9). This is an intriguing prayer, because God is already holy; he cannot be holier. So what does it mean? It appears that it must be translated: "may we sanctify your name." This makes strong sense in Jewish mentality because hallowing God's name is "the most characteristic feature of Jewish ethics."[19] In fact, one of the unspoken rules of Jewish life is that one must never profane the Lord's name before Gentiles. The responsibility falls on us. The early fathers Cyprian and Chrysostom made this important point.[20] By our lives—our dealing with others, our decision-making, our actions, our words, our dispositions, our lifestyles, and everything we do—we sanctify the name of our Lord. The prayer, thus, is "May we live our lives blamelessly so that your name is sanctified, glorified, and made known to all." This is the essence of the command of Jesus in Matthew 5:16: "Let your light shine before others, that they may see your good deeds and glorify your Father in heaven."

Reformations and Innovations

God remained true to his promise of restoration. After several decades of exile, the Persians allowed the Israelites to migrate back to Palestine. A genuine revival occurred among the people when they returned. Filled with religious zeal, they immediately set to rebuild the walls, build the temple, and institute changes in politics, religious observances, and worship. Massive re-organization took place to prevent the mistakes of pre-exilic Israel from happening again, especially idolatry. With the memory of their deposition, they worked towards radical transformation and called for nonconformity with the mistakes of their predecessors.[21] In fact, Ezekiel talked about watchmen whose responsibility was to warn people of their wicked ways (33:7–9). Prophets of judgment who were marginalized in the

---

19. Keener, *A Commentary on the Gospel of Matthew*, 219.
20. Simonetti, *Matthew 1–13*, 132–33.
21. Smith-Christopher, *A Biblical Theology of Exile*, 120–22.

pre-exilic era gained favorable place in the hearts of the people.[22] They will not turn a deaf ear to God's warnings again. Several concrete reformations during the post-exilic era deserve our attention, because they reveal the changed mindset of the people in response to God's saving grace. The Israelites finally realized the importance of mutual reciprocity in the divine-human relationship. Innovations were instituted as human counterparts in the covenant partnership.

Re-organization of Temple Leadership. Recognizing that the kings were predominantly responsible for national idolatry and apostasy in the pre-exilic era, the priestly leaders determined that the temple need to be detached from the auspices of the monarchy. This was a radical break from the tradition that David and Solomon started. This meant, however that sacrificial offerings should no longer be provided by political leaders and a new way of providing for the priest—instead of state support—needed to be instituted.[23] In addition, to ensure the sanctity of the temple, laity (including the king) were not allowed to perform priestly functions or enter spaces designated only for priests. Worship, not political governance, should determine the future of God's people.

Strengthening of Family Kinship. The people needed to relinquish the old system. This applied especially to the end of monarchy and the beginning of greater emphasis upon smaller units of social cohesion, like the family.[24] Politically, the Persians did not allow kings in their colonies, but theologically, "the holy apparatus has ended because Yahweh, its guarantor, had become its enemy."[25] The loss of hegemonic political authority gave impetus to the emergence of decentralized forms of organization based on kinship. This is an important development, because the responsibility of transmitting the law and the expectations of the covenant to future generation fell upon the family. Active individual and collective participation in their religion became crucial. This also signifies the shift from mere religious performance in a centralized location to bringing religious observances at home.

Awareness of Social Boundaries. The end of the monarchy implied a restructuring of the political and social institutions of Israel. This included a

---

22. Albertz, *A History of Israelite Religion*, 370.
23. Albertz, *A History of Israelite Religion*, 432.
24. See Ackyord, *Exile and Restoration*, 60–61, where the author presents Jeremiah's wish for the restoration of Davidic house and righteous rulers (Jer 30:9; 33:14–18).
25. Brueggemann, *Hopeful Imagination*, 32.

new awareness of their distinct identity as the people of God. The Israelites in the pre-exilic era understood their identity in relation to the Egyptian deliverance and the covenant. This inward-looking self-identification as God's chosen people gave them a false sense of security that God would not abandon them amidst their insolence. But because the exile was largely caused by flirting with other cultures and religions, the post-exilic period saw a tightening of social boundaries. They became xenophobic, nationalistic, and ethnocentric. The Israelites separated themselves from foreigners (Ezra 6:21; 9:1; 10:8; Neh 9:2; 10:29; 13:3), even going so far as putting away their foreign wives and children (Ezra 10:1–7).[26] Smith-Christopher enumerates two prevalent mentalities: (1) a strong sense of identity that is separate from those traditions and cultures that surround them, and (2) the necessity to maintain their social boundaries, that is, to protect their unique identity through a strong emphasis on internal solidarity and consistency.[27] The stories of Daniel taught the importance of courageous resistance to external influences for the sake of maintaining one's identity as a Jew, even at the cost of one's life.

Emphasis on Religious Purity. Along with establishing clear social boundaries, the Israelites also tightened their religious practices to ensure purity. This meant regulating boundaries that made clear distinction between the clean and unclean. Aware that their pre-exilic sin included profaning holy things, the people resolved to take the command to be separate more literally from abominations associated with foreign practices (Lev 18:24–30). The reform of Nehemiah included the purification of the priests and the Levites "of everything foreign" (Neh 13:29–30). Daniel again became the model of purity for his refusal to pollute himself with Babylonian food. Even the prohibition of laity performing priestly duties is related here, because the holy things and places of the temple must not be defiled by unconsecrated hands.

Conclusions

The exile reveals both the judgment of God against sinners and his gracious initiative to restore them to himself. The cycle of blessing and punishment might appear tiresome for readers, but the narrative depicts the relationship between human innate incapability and divine gracious sovereignty.

---

26. Kaiser, *A History of Israel*, 441–42.
27. Smith-Christopher, *A Biblical Theology of Exile*, 138.

Restoration and Renewal

The exile and its despair are God's righteous No to sin, but we are glad that the story is followed by promises and fulfilment of a restoration that involve both undoing the past and empowerment for the future. The exile made the Israelites realize many things, including the importance of their active responsibility as worshipping holy people. Their post-exilic reform programs reveal their newly-found and deep-seated zeal to be the people they ought to be. Their awareness was deepened about who God is and what he expects from them as his covenant partners.

The cosmic scope of God's movement in salvation history is also reaffirmed in the exilic narrative. God's governance extends to all nations, since creation is his. He is free to utilize all earthly political powers for his purposes, whether they be for destruction (Babylon, Jer 20:4) or for restoration (Persia, Isa 45:1). The oracles of judgment insinuate that punishment awaits every nation that opposes God. The scope of God's involvement is not limited to the covenant people. As Brueggemann writes, the exilic narrative "corrects the easy impression that the Old Testament is singularly preoccupied with Yahweh's powerful commitment to Israel . . . This claim of centrality for Israel needs to be sharply qualified. Israel does not live in a sociological vacuum . . . Yahweh has a rich field of engagement with the nations."[28] The arena of God's saving work is the whole of world history that started in Genesis. This is important to remember as we begin to shift our attention to the saving work of God in the New Testament.

---

28. Brueggemann, *Theology of the Old Testament*, 525.

6

Grace and Truth

> "For God so loved the world that he gave his one and only Son, that whoever believes in him shall not perish but have eternal life. For God did not send his Son into the world to condemn the world, but to save the world through him"
>
> —JOHN 3:16–17

SOME NEW TESTAMENT SCHOLARS jest that the Old Testament is a long Preface to the real stuff of the Bible. The witticism does not warrant vindication, but there is truism in it. It is only when we come to the New Testament that full understanding of grace and salvation happens. In this chapter, we find the redemptive work of God reaching culmination in the incarnation of his Son. This does not happen in a vacuum. The whole creation narrative, along with Yahweh's special treatment of the Israelites, constitutes the whole background of the work of the God-man savior. Although Israelite history is not rose-colored, it provides us with the tools to understand the work of Jesus Christ. For instance, apart from the concept of election of one for the sake of the many, blood and sacrifice, and the idea of mediated divine blessing, we will not be able to appreciate who Jesus is and what he accomplished for us. These themes are important, first, because they lead to an awareness that Israel as a nation is the God-appointed womb out of which metaphors of salvation are forged, and second, because they provide the necessary background in understanding the salvific life and ministry of Jesus Christ.

Challenging the Symbols of Israel

As New Testament scholar Rob van Houwelingen asserts, "God is oriented to Israel . . . Israel remains his point of departure."[1] In particular, the post-exilic era occupies an important place.[2] Having experienced the ramifications of disobedience to the stipulations of the covenant, the Israelites vowed to be a better people of God. Unfortunately, although Israel's post-exilic renewals are noteworthy, they also became the primary reason for the nation's religious bankruptcy in the first century. The various well-loved symbols of temple, land, family, and Sabbath served as ends in themselves. Their rigid understanding of purity implicitly produced outcasts. This is because "a society that insisted angrily on its own purity toward outsiders," N. T. Wright writes, "would also maintain sharp distinctions, and perpetuate economic and other injustices, within itself."[3] The rebuilt temple, which was supposedly the symbol and place of forgiveness and reconciliation with Yahweh, represented the "elitist, exclusivist, and centralist point of view."[4] Eschatological expectations of deliverance closely tied with nationalistic agenda intensified their convictions about their privileged status as God's chosen people. When this is married to their hardened imposition of social boundaries for the sake of maintaining religious purity, they became a closed community that neglected their missionary calling to the world. Wright expresses the Jewish circumstance at the time of the incarnation: "The larger biblical narrative indicated that the fate of humankind as a whole was hanging upon the rescue operation that has been launched in the family of Abraham, but that was now itself, in peril."[5]

Jesus came at a time when the longings of the Jews for salvation was at a boiling point. The concern of the Jewish leaders was ultimately holiness, but their nationalistic and political dreams skewed their understanding of salvation. They longed for a messiah king who would overthrow current oppressive powers that contaminated the land. This justified the use of

1. van Houwelingen, "The Redemptive-Historical Dynamics of the Salvation," 308.
2. Lee, "Now Is the Acceptable Time," 1–13.
3. Borg and Wright, *The Meaning of Jesus*, 36.
4. van der Platt, *Salvation in the NT*, 157.
5. Wright, *The Day the Revolution Began*, 106.

violence. Jesus, on the other hand, "denounced the use of military action, and he advocated the deeper revolution of loving one's enemies, taking up one's cross, and losing one's life in order to gain it."[6] Jesus was conscious of his messianic vocation but his agenda and methods in establishing the kingdom deviated from his contemporaries' expectations. His conflict with the religious leaders was unavoidable because his message and actions repeatedly challenged many Jewish heartfelt convictions concerning their identity and action as the holy people of God. As God himself acting in the world, Jesus boldly claimed that their religious symbols and apparatuses have been rendered obsolete by his arrival.[7] They were not bad in themselves but have just become unnecessary. He is now the Lord of the Sabbath (Matt 12:8; Mark 2:27–28), whose mission was to do good works out of love (Matt 12:12). Family kinship and covenant identity are no longer grounded in blood relations to Abraham but are found in being gathered around Jesus as his obedient brothers and sisters (Matt 12:50; Mark 3:35). The existing temple is under judgment for its impurity and oppressive legalistic demands. Jesus constituted the new temple, the mobile place of forgiveness and reconciliation.

Salvation in Christ

There is continuity between the promises of the prophets and the coming of Jesus Christ. If Wright is correct that the primary need of the Jewish people is "from one point of view, 'the end of exile,' and from another point of view, 'forgiveness of sins,'" then the coming of Jesus is crucial.[8] The genealogy of Matthew 1:1–17 emphatically asserts that the coming of Jesus stands in line with God's purposes since the calling of Abraham. That Jesus "will save his people from their sins" (Acts 1:21) signifies the end of the exile from within Israel to the nations. This is a major claim. God is doing something new and radical, beginning with Israel and to the world. Naming Jesus as Savior (1:21) right at the very beginning of the New Testament introduces him and his soteriological vocation. It is not surprising then, that the Gospels narrate "a Christological story, cloaked in soteriological robe."[9] Salvation is exclusively found in Jesus

---

6. Borg and Wright, *The Meaning of Jesus*, 96.
7. Wright, *The Challenge of Jesus*, 58–73.
8. Wright, *The Day the Revolution Began*, 138.
9. Platt, *Salvation in the NT*, 68.

(Heb 4:12; 5:31; 13:38; 15:11). He is the pioneer (Heb 2:10), source (Heb 5:9), and mediator of complete salvation (Heb 7:25).

Salvific Person: Who is Jesus?

The tendency of modern scholarship is to approach the question of the identity of Jesus from a *functional perspective*, i.e., who Jesus is in the light of what he does, or a *cultural perspective*, i.e., who Jesus is in the light of Jewish history. These have their own merits, but they lean more towards emphasizing the historical Jesus at the expense of the theological Jesus. In particular, his trinitarian identity is eclipsed. The identity of Jesus, if approached from a *relational perspective*, provides a picture of a person-in-relation. The Gospels do not present an individualistic and detached Christ. In fact, Jesus is referred to as "Jesus of Nazareth" (John 18:5), "son of Joseph" (John 1:45), or "the Holy One of God" (Mark 1:24). For the Gospel writers, Jesus' identity is not a matter of *being as* (a self-existing individual) but a *being with* (a person-in-relation). Therefore, we cannot really understand Jesus and his salvific work apart from the Father and the Holy Spirit.

First, Jesus is the obedient Son of the Father who sent him to the world with a mission (John 3:16–17; 6:38; 20:21). Jesus unashamedly confessed that he does the will of the Father who sent him (John 4:34). He keeps the Father's commands (John 15:10) not only in his redemptive acts, but also in his revealing work. "I do not speak on my own," Jesus asserts, "but the Father who sent me commanded me to say all that I have spoken . . . So whatever I say is just what the Father has told me to say" (John 12:49–50). Jesus was conscious that he was sent into the world by the Father to save it (John 3:16–17). He knew that through him "God was reconciling the world to himself" (2 Cor 5:19). God wants to establish a new covenant through the Anointed One, and his target is not just a person (e.g., Abraham) or a nation (e.g., Israel). He wants to offer forgiveness to all and bring all creation back to intimate relationship with him. The cosmic scope of Jesus' salvific work is expressed throughout the New Testament. It is true that he is "the glory of your people Israel," but he also came as "a light to the Gentiles" (Luke 2:32).

Second, Jesus is fully human dependent on the Holy Spirit. This addresses the how of his whole-life obedience. He was conceived by the Spirit (Matt 1:20; Luke 1:35), baptized with the Spirit (Matt 3:16; Mark 1:10), led by the Spirit (Matt 4:1; Mark 1:12; Luke 4:1), anointed by the Spirit to preach and minister (Luke 4:14, 18–19), and raised from the dead in the power of the Spirit (1 Pet 3:18). Even his exorcisms are in the power of the Spirit (Matt 12:28). Jesus is the *Christos*, whose life and ministry are permeated through and through by the Spirit. As John R. Coulson writes, "Christ is able to have a relationship with God, to live in obedience, and to fulfill his messianic mission only because he has God's Spirit indwelling and empowering him."[10] This is important because although divinity is not an expected messianic trait, being anointed by the Spirit is. It is also significant for us today because the work of the Spirit in the fully human Jesus is the pattern of his enabling work to us as the people of God called to be a royal priesthood (1 Pet 2:9).

Nevertheless, Jerome H. Neyrey asserts that Jesus should be seen in the light of his own culture.[11] It is important to recognize that Jesus is truly born of out of the womb of Israel. This means that Jesus is who he is and what he does precisely because he is a Jew. He comes from a rich history that involves (1) the calling of Abraham and his descendants to be a blessing, (2) the establishment of covenants that involved stipulations for holy life, (3) the giving of the law, grounded in love, that serves to guide God's people toward healthy relationship with him and with others, (4) the centrality of religious customs and worship practices for the forgiveness of sins and toward reconciliation with God, (5) the stories of national deliverance, redemption, and renewal through God's anointed servants, and (6) the missionary calling of the chosen people of God to the world. Of course, Jesus' saving mission is more than Jewish in its scope. He comes both as a Jew to fulfill God's promise to Abraham to bless all the nations through his descendants and as the incarnate Son of God to restore human beings in his image and in their vocation to all creation.

Salvific Message: The Kingdom of God

Jesus acted as an authoritative preacher and teacher whose primary proclamation is the kingdom of God breaking into history (Matt 3:2; 4:7; Mark 1:15). His iconic Sermon on the Mount centered on the kingdom, expressed in many different parables. But what is the kingdom all about? For Calvin L. Porter, it is "God-ruling" that brings about salvation.[12] Wright agrees. The

10. Coulson, "Jesus and the Spirit in Paul's Theology," 95.
11. See his book *Imagining Jesus in His Own Culture*.
12. Porter, "The Salvation Story in the New Testament," 154.

kingdom of heaven, as often used in the Gospel of Matthew, "refers to the rule of heaven, that is, God, being brought to bear in the present world."[13] This is not a militaristic reality. The real enemy is not political oppressors, but sin and evil. Hence, the kingdom Jesus proclaimed would not emerge after the gruesome death of their enemies. Instead, it would come through humility, self-denial, and love. This was Jesus' radical alternative.

> He was telling his hearers . . . to give up their agendas and to trust him for his way of being Israel, his way of bringing the kingdom, his kingdom agenda. In particular, he was urging them . . . to abandon their crazy dreams of nationalistic revolution . . . Jesus was opposed to it because he saw it as, paradoxically, a way of being deeply disloyal to Israel's God: specifically, to Israel's vocation to be the light of the world . . . Jesus was offering as a counter-agenda an utterly risky way of being Israel, the way of turning the other cheek and going the second mile, the way of losing your life to gain it, the way of new community in which debts and sins were to be forgiven.[14]

Jesus' announced kingdom is characterized not by righteous bloodshed or violence. He invited the Jews to a new way of seeing reality, a new way of centering their existence in God, and a new way of living in godly ethics and social vision.[15] He was offering a kingdom where the covenant people of God live as gracious people renewed by God's Word and by the Spirit, whose fruit is love. If they were to be a blessing to the nations, they would need to let go of their hatred and prejudice, and learn to forgive. It is only by being generous to their enemies that they can reflect God's character and convince them to join them in his worship. Their mission should follow after God's: not to condemn but to save the world (John 3:17).

Salvific Challenge: Repentance

When Jesus proclaimed the kingdom, Wright argues, he did so in four sequential moves: invitation, welcome, challenge, and summons. He invited everyone to listen and be a part of the new Israel. He welcomed everyone to himself. He challenged people "to live as the new covenant people, the returned-from-exile people, the people whose hearts were renewed by the

13. Wright, *The Challenge of Jesus*, 36–37.
14. Borg and Wright, *The Meaning of Jesus*, 38.
15. Borg and Wright, *The Meaning of Jesus*, 69–70.

word and work of the living God."[16] He summoned them to a renewed mind, where they realize the concerns of God and pursue the kingdom of righteousness, peace, and joy (Rom 14:17) through self-denial and servitude, not defiance and violence. At the center of these is the call to repentance (Matt 3:2; 4:17; Mark 1:15) and belief in him (Matt 10:40; Mark 9:23; John 5:24; 20:31). Hence, although salvation is God's gracious initiative and contains elements that he alone can accomplish for us (e.g., defeating evil and forgiveness of sins), he demanded appropriate responses from his audience.

The evangelistic crusade movement, which emphasizes instantaneous conversion in public gathering, has reduced repentance to "accepting Jesus as Lord and Savior." This was not what Jesus meant when he admonished people to repent. What Jesus did was to summon his hearers "to give up their whole way of life, their national and social agenda, and to trust him for a different agenda, a different set of goals."[17] "The key thing," Wright asserts, "was that the inbreaking of the kingdom Jesus was announcing created a new world, a new context, and he was challenging his hearers to become the new people that this new context demanded . . . He was offering a challenge to his contemporaries to a way of life, a way of forgiveness and prayer, a way of jubilee."[18] The Sermon on the Mount, with its radical proposals and reinterpretations of the known law ("You have heard it was said, but now I say . . . Matt 5:21–48) epitomizes Jesus' radical new proposal. He was calling people to *metanoia*, a change of mindset about their identity and ethics as the people of God.

John the Baptist preached "a baptism of repentance for the forgiveness of sins" (Mark 1:4). If baptism is for God-fearing Gentiles who desire to become proselyte members of the people of God,[19] then the Baptist's message sounded strange to Jewish audience, who, by blood relation to Abraham, are already the people of God. Both John and Jesus offered a critique from within and were suggesting that contrary to the Jews' expectation of God's judgment to their nation's enemies, they too are under judgment. They too needed to repent. Blood relations do not exempt them from judgment. By virtue of their disobedience, Jesus proclaimed, they are illegitimate children of Abraham (John 8:39–40). If the Jews were to be saved, they had to change their view of God as seen and met in Jesus. "Salvific faith involves

---

16. Borg and Wright, *The Meaning of Jesus*, 39.
17. Borg and Wright, *The Meaning of Jesus*, 27.
18. Borg and Wright, *The Meaning of Jesus*, 46.
19. Torrance, "Proselyte Baptism," 150–54.

full acceptance of the message of Jesus as well as his person, which includes his identity and his origin from God as Agent."[20] Jesus challenges us to put our faith in him as the Son of the Father, sent to us for our salvation (John 1:18; 10:30; 6:46; 3:16; 6:40; 12:49–50). No one can remain neutral, because "to be absolutely neutral before God is to be absolutely hostile to God."[21]

Salvation Recipient: All are Invited

The point of Jesus' life and mission is that salvation is by lavish grace. Because of the rigidity of the law imposed by Jewish religious demands, real belongingness to the people of God required ticking off a set of boxes for qualifications. Many naturally fell short. Within the people of God, by virtue of their defects, many were treated as second class citizens. Gentiles found it even harder to be included; they were threats to the avoided or defeated. To remain blessed as a nation, the Israelites forgot their calling to be blessing to the nations. Jesus' mission of inclusion entails the redemption of the gospel message from its oppressive stewards. The Israelites have not only forgotten their mandate as a kingdom of priests who would reveal God's love and holiness through their history. They have also corrupted it with their own ethnocentric vision. In his exhortation and life, Jesus called the Israelites back to the original intention of the Abrahamic covenant. He re-opened the invitation for all to be blessed. The Ethiopian eunuch is a case in point (Acts 8:26–40). As a eunuch, he would have been excluded from temple worship (see Deut 23:1–3). Although Isaiah envisioned their inclusion in the last days (56:4–6), the temple would have its door closed for them in the first century. Philip's action thus symbolizes that the physically mutilated—even those beyond physical restoration—are welcome in the kingdom of God.

Jesus is the mediator who reconciles all of humanity with God (1 Tim 2:5). He is the Savior of the whole world (John 3:16). This was what the Israelites missed. The Messiah does not serve only the Jews; he is the fulfillment of the universal blessing God willed for creation and expressed specially in the Abrahamic covenant of blessing to the nations. In the words of Simeon, Jesus is the "light for revelation to the Gentiles and for the glory to your people Israel" (Luke 2:32). Through him "all people will see God's salvation" (Luke 3:6). The "mystery that has been kept hidden" is revealed

---

20. Platt, *Salvation in the NT,* 120.
21. Torrance, *Persons in Communion,* 12–15.

through the coming of Jesus Christ: that Gentiles share "the glorious riches of this mystery, which is Christ in you" (Col 1:26–27; Eph 3:8–9). Jesus is the perfect son of Abraham who blesses the nations through his word and deed. In Christ, therefore, the calling of Israel to become blessing to the nations is fulfilled. His saving work is indeed "according to the Scriptures" (1 Cor 15:3), because he fulfills the law and its requirements in its application to all people (Matt 5:17).

Salvation from Sin

Although Jesus operated in a Jewish context, his salvific work had different emphases than his contemporary religious leaders. Jesus' death may be politically attributed as the culminating result of these significant differences. First, in contrast to a primarily political view of salvation, Jesus' offer of salvation was holistic. His miracles, although mostly physical in nature, reveal his concern for people's *shalom*. True restoration meant social reintegration and religious reinstatement. Second, because Jesus' agenda was not political, he discredited a militaristic crusade toward liberation, and instead proposed the way of peace, humility, gentleness, and sacrifice. Ironically, his pacifist methods were met with strong resistance because they challenged existing norms and expectations. To a large degree, non-aggression is not violent to the enemies, but is violent to the self. It asks for the abandonment of our prerogative to vengeance and allows others to abuse our graciousness.

Third, and most importantly, Jesus focused on addressing a different problem: the problem of sin—in the world and within Israel itself. The kingdom of God, Paul writes, is concerned more with the "powers of this dark world" and "the spiritual forces of evil" (Eph 6:12). Behind the present human condition is the fundamental reality of sin. The Jews viewed themselves as the privileged people of God; they felt exempted from the problem. Sinners primarily referred to others. Jesus' calling toward the Jews to repent, therefore, shocked them. Moreover, contrary to the vision of the Jews where sinners suffer at the righteous hand of God for their wickedness, Jesus taught that sinners are invited to the kingdom of God too. This was the point of the parable of the prodigal son. The older brother represents the Jews who think that those who err should be punished. He was furious when his prodigal brother was welcomed home by his father and was even treated with honor. The gracious words of the forgiving father

Grace and Truth

reveal the heart of God for the entire world: "You are always with me, and everything I have is yours. But we had to celebrate and be glad, because this brother of yours was dead and is alive again; he was lost and is found" (Luke 15:31–32). The Gospel offers forgiveness, not condemnation of sinners. The kingdom banquet invites all who have fallen short of the glory of God and those who have gone astray.

Forgiveness is an important blessing of the kingdom. It can mean remission of monetary debt, freedom from bondage, or pardon from sin (Matt 6:14–15; Mark 2:5–10; Luke 7:47–50). Throughout his itinerant ministry, Jesus forgave others (Luke 7:47–48). The combination of healing and forgiveness of sins symbolizes the kingdom's holistic interest and emphasis (Matt 9:2; Mark 2:5–7). Because illness was considered as the consequence of sin, healing entailed divine forgiveness for the family or the sick, or both. Furthermore, because the exile is the consequence of sin, forgiveness of sins entails the end of exile. The banished or the scattered may come back to God not through their own effort, but through God's gracious forgiveness.

It may be argued that Jesus had a deeper vision of salvation than his contemporaries. The Jews inherited the tradition of the Old Testament, where many allusions to salvation are physical and political, like deliverance from oppressors or enemies (Exod 3:7–8; Judg 2:15–16, 18), victory in battle (Ps 20:6–9; 33:16–19), healing of sickness (Isa 38:20), rescue from personal enemies, persecutors, detractors (Ps 7:1–2, 10; Jer 15:20–21), and vindication in court (Ps 72:4, 13; 76:8–9).[22] Of course, the New Testament does not abandon these for a purely spiritual view of salvation. What Jesus did was to re-emphasize what his contemporaries blindly neglected. Ben Witherington argued that there is a noticeable progression toward a more spiritual understanding of salvation from Luke to Acts.[23] This means that the Israelite nationalistic-political notion of salvation was deemed lacking in perspective by New Testament writers. Their interaction with Jesus changed their nationalistic views to include the deeper realities of sin and death that Jesus came to deal with. After all, Jesus reveals true knowledge of salvation "through the forgiveness of sins" (Luke 1:77). He was announced to "save his people from their sins" (Matt 1:21). In emphasizing salvation from sin, Jesus was bringing the Jews back beyond the calling of Abraham

22. Wright, *Salvation Belongs to Our God*, 3–6.
23. Witherington, "Salvation and Health in Christianity Antiquity," 154. King agrees with Witherington, but argues that the progression is more from the OT to the NT, because a spiritual view of salvation is already salient in Luke's Gospel. See King, "The Progressive Announcement of Salvation in Luke," 5–28.

to the fall of the first humans. He was asking them to abandon their nationalistic aspirations and see their place in God's cosmic plans.

Conclusions

The history of salvation that begun in creation reaches a definitive moment in God's sending of the incarnate Son in the world (John 3:16–17). As God's tangible presence and response to humanity's long predicament, Jesus lived and labored in a specific time and space. In particular, he was born out of the womb of Israel. This makes his salvific life and work deeply rooted in history. His life and work must be understood in the light of his own political, social, and religious contexts. In this chapter, we sought to understand "the grace of the Lord Jesus Christ" by locating him within the hopes and aspirations of the Jews, whose immediate background is the exile. Jesus spoke as a prophet who called the Israelites back to God's agenda, challenged their cherished national symbols of identity, questioned their understanding of holiness, rejected their ideologies and applications of purity laws, and reinterpreted their laws so that they become aligned with God's own agenda. He announced himself as God's own presence, offering forgiveness and restoration to those who will repent and believe. He proclaimed an inclusive kingdom for all. He offered holistic salvation that included physical renewal, social reintegration, forgiveness of sins, and reconciliation with God. He modeled kingdom values of humility, love, and sacrifice.

7

Embodied Saving Grace

"For you know the grace of our Lord Jesus Christ, that though he was rich, yet for your sake he became poor, so that you through his poverty might become rich"

—2 CORINTHIANS 8:9

JESUS' MESSAGE, CHALLENGE, AND approach are closely linked to the immediate historical events of his time. This is why the previous chapter, concentrating primarily on the four Gospels, locates Jesus Christ in the context of Israel's cyclic history of rebellion-punishment-renewal. In particular, Jewish longings for salvation and the Messiah help us understand his teachings about the kingdom and his call to repentance. However, this does not mean that Jesus' salvific work is limited to addressing Jewish expectations. He is after all *Yeshua*, the savior of the world. He is the incarnate Son whose saving mission is part of the story of God's grace that began with creation. Thus, although the immediate context of Jesus' life and work is Jewish history and life, the range of his redemptive work is cosmic.

Grace and Salvation

The One Mediator

The universal work of Christ is grounded in the fact that he is also the head of creation. All of creation is in him and for him (Col 1:16). The audacity of this claim surely rattled Jews and Gentiles alike in the first century, but Christians remained true to their faith affirmation that "salvation is found in no one else, for there is no other name under heaven given to mankind by which we must be saved" (Acts 4:12). Jesus is the only way to salvation (John 14:6), the only mediator between God and humanity (1 Tim 2:5). In his speech to the Athenians, Paul proclaims that ignorance of this is no longer acceptable, because God has appointed Jesus Christ, the one he raised from the dead, to judge the world (Acts 17:30–31). Paul's successful mission to the Gentiles indicates that the saving work of Christ is not only for the Jews, but for all (2 Cor 5:14–15). Jesus' saving work, therefore, is the ultimate fulfillment of the promise of Yahweh to Abraham that nations will be blessed through him and his descendants (Gen 12:1–3). The universal story of God's work which began in creation, along with his purposes of human communion and vocation, reaches beautiful culmination in the coming of the incarnate Son to redeem, reconcile, and recreate humanity. Israel as a nation may have failed in their missional vocation, but it is also from within Israel that God fulfills his covenant promise to bless all of humanity.

But how is the coming of the incarnate Son God's gracious and saving act? Before we respond to this, it must be noted that the need for salvation is rooted in the perennial problem of sin and its consequence: death. According to New Testament scholar N. T. Wright, sin must not be understood only morally or ethically, or in terms of do's and don'ts. It is essentially "the failure to be fully functioning, God-reflecting human beings."[1] Sin is both a matter of commission and omission. Jesus' saving work to bring forgiveness of sins entails the undoing of sin and its effects, and providing new humanity for all. The end of exile (theologically understood), pardon from sins, the restoration of humanity in reconciled relationship with God, and the renewal of God's image in humanity are all aspects of Christ's redeeming work. Moreover, in Christ, we are saved from the guilt of past sins, the present power of sin, and the fear of future punishment.[2]

Because sin has personal, social, and cosmic effects, Jesus' saving work is also comprehensive. The coming of Jesus Christ is the inauguration of

---

1. Wright, *The Day the Revolution Began*, 268.
2. Oden, *John Wesley's Scriptural Christianity*, 192–93.

God's kingdom on earth, the ultimate defeat of evil, and the renewal of the entire cosmos and its inhabitant to their God-given purpose and calling. The incarnation, therefore, is God's decisive saving movement. God himself becomes one of us, with us, and for us. Grace is God's gift of himself acting on our behalf and for us amid our abject predicament. In his downward movement he becomes human so that he can take humans back to God in his upward movement. This is how God decides to save us. The only way to the Father is through Jesus Christ (John 14:6). When we want to understand what salvation is and how it is accomplished for us, we have to look closely at the entire life of Jesus.

Incarnation and Salvation

What is the saving grace of Jesus? Paul responds: "For you know the grace of our Lord Jesus Christ, that though he was rich, yet for your sake he became poor, so that you through his poverty might become rich" (2 Cor 8:9). The same affirmation may be found in Philippians 2:6–11, the so-called hymn of Christ's humiliation and exaltation. To save us, the Son of God had to go through divine self-emptying and abasement—even to death—in order to reconcile us to God. In these passages, we see the unity and tension between the divine and human natures of the incarnate Son. The New Testament highlights the integrity of both.

It is imperative that Jesus is God, for only God can save: "Who can forgive sins but God alone?" (Mark 2:7). The assurance of our salvation rests in the fact that the action and word of Jesus are the act and word of God himself. Whoever Jesus proclaims to be forgiven is indeed forgiven. St. Athanasius (c. 293–373) succinctly wrote, "If Jesus Christ is not himself God, then there is no final authority or validity for anything he said or did for human beings. If he were not divine, he could not act divinely . . . No creature can ever be saved by a creature."[3] If Jesus is not God and we face God in the final judgment, we would have no confidence about our salvation, because we would have been saved by a mere human prophet or messenger. But because the Savior is himself the Judge, we can boldly come before God, knowing fully well that no higher entity may question his saving work for us. The saving activity of Jesus is the saving activity of God.

It is equally important that Jesus is human, for he cannot represent us to God without being so. Our salvation is not only worked out by God

---

3. Athanasius, *Contra Arius*, II.21–31; in NPNF2 4: 359–65.

in Christ, but also by humanity in Christ. For the writer of Hebrews, the humanity of Christ is a necessary component of his saving work. He had to be "fully human in every way, in order that he might become a merciful and faithful high priest in service to God, and that he might make atonement for the sins of the people" (Heb 2:17). In short, "Jesus' incarnation provides the source for 'full salvation.'"[4] Here we come to grips with the concepts of representation and substitution. We will unpack this more in the following sections. Suffice it for now to say that Jesus stands as one for the many, experiencing on our behalf what we could not bear for ourselves.

Unfortunately, as John Deschner observes, "one of the problems of Wesleyan Christology" is "the lack of emphasis on the human nature of Christ."[5] A serious reflection on how the entire life of Christ is salvific is too often missing in Wesleyan literature. Tom Noble's attempt to ground sanctification in the incarnation in *Holy Trinity, Holy People* provides a template that may be applied to the doctrine of salvation, which I follow in this chapter.[6] This is important, because we must consider that Jesus is savior from his birth. Our tendency to focus on the death of Jesus Christ negatively implies that everything before the cross is secondary in significance, because they are mere preparatory events. This cannot be. We need to re-discover the patristic emphasis on the saving life of Jesus Christ, particularly his humanity. Augustine, for instance, wrote that Jesus "applied to us the similarity of his humanity to take away the dissimilarity of our iniquity, and becoming of our mortality he made us partakers of his divinity."[7] Theologians have referred to this as Christ's atoning exchange. He takes what is ours so that we may receive what is his. Echoing 2 Corinthians 8:9, Gregory of Nazianzus also wrote, "He Who gives riches becomes poor, for He assumes the poverty of my flesh, that I may assume the riches of His Godhead. He that is full empties Himself, for He empties Himself of His glory for a short while, that I may have a share in His Fullness."[8]

---

4. For a lengthier elaboration of this important verse in our salvation, see Ackerman, "The High Priesthood of Jesus," 226–45. See also Gschwandtner, "Sharing Our Weakness," 164–78, for the role of the humanity of Christ in salvation.

5. Deschner, *Wesley's Christology*, 24.

6. Noble, *Holy Trinity, Holy People*, 158–79.

7. Quoted in Crawford, "Pursuing an Ontology of Attunement through St. Augustine's Christology," 189.

8. Gregory of Nazianzus, "On the Theophany, or Birthday of Christ," in *NPNF2* 7: 349.

The Saving Grace of Christ's Life

We must see Jesus Christ "not only as the embodiment of God's pardoning and empowering initiative toward us, but also as the embodiment of humanity's ideal reception of and response to that divine initiative."[9] Salvation is not only the work of God in Christ for us, but also humanity's response in Christ for us. As humanity's representative and substitute, Jesus Christ obediently lives out what it means to be human. He embodies our concerns and responds to God's righteous will from the depths of his participation in our humanity.

The virgin birth marks the beginning of the incarnate Son's saving work. It powerfully teaches us that salvation is solely God's initiative. His birth was announced to Mary, who was chosen out of sheer divine grace and freedom. Her response is instructive about how we too may respond to God's work: "May it be to me as you have said" (Luke 1:38). What is crucial in the birth of Jesus is the inauguration of a new humanity, marking a significant break from the sinful humanity we have inherited from Adam. As Paul stated in Romans 5:12–21, Jesus Christ is the new Adam upon which our human identity and destiny now rest. God does not recreate humanity out of nothing; in Christ and by the Spirit he recreates us from within present human existence. The parallelism between Adam and Jesus is unmistakable. In the same way that Adam was given life by the divine breath (Gen 2:7), Jesus is conceived by the Holy Spirit (Luke 1:35). But the second Adam obediently succeeds where the first Adam failed. Through Adam, humanity died, but through Christ's obedience we receive grace and life (Rom 5:15). In Adam there is condemnation and judgment, but in Christ there is pardon (Rom 5:16, 18). In Adam there is sin and death, but in Christ there is "provision of grace and the gift of righteousness" (Rom 5:17). In Adam's disobedience sin came to all, but in Christ's obedience "many will be made righteousness" (Rom 5:19). The birth of Christ spells the redemption of humanity because at last, the true human appeared.

Luke tells us that Jesus grew in wisdom and stature, and that the grace of God was upon him (2:40, 52). This brief summary of Jesus' childhood vividly portrays Jesus' full humanity. Like the rest of us, Jesus developed and matured gradually. But what does this have to do with our salvation? As the firstborn (Col 1:15) Jesus inaugurates a new humanity by assuming and living it first, so that humanity may also understand and experience

---

9. Hambrick and Lodahl, "Responsible Grace in Christology?" 100.

what true humanity looks like. He does this for us as an example also. He assumed our humanity, "being made in human likeness" to save us (Phil 2:7). Second-century theologian Irenaeus summarizes this well:

> He came to save all through the means of Himself—all, I say, who through Him are born again to God—infants, and children, and boys, and youths, and old men. He therefore passed through every age, becoming an infant for infants, thus sanctifying infants; a child for children, thus sanctifying those who are of this age, being at the same time made to them an example of piety, righteousness, and submission; a youth for youths, becoming an example to youths, and thus sanctifying them for the Lord. So likewise He was an old man for old men, that He might be a perfect Master for all, not merely as respects the setting forth of the truth, but also as regards age, sanctifying at the same time the aged also, and becoming an example to them likewise. Then, at last, He came on to death itself, that He might be "the first-born from the dead, that in all things He might have the pre-eminence," the Prince of life, existing before all, and going before all.[10]

Hebrews 5:8 closely links Jesus growth and his saving work: "He learned obedience from what he suffered and, once made perfect, he became the source of eternal salvation for all who obey him." The salvific work of Jesus is marked by suffering, not only at the cross but throughout his life. Karl Barth is worth quoting at length:

> This man is persecuted all His life, a stranger in His own family . . . and in His nation; a stranger in the spheres of the State and Church and civilization. And what a road of manifest ill-success He treads! In what utter loneliness and temptation He stands among men, the leaders of His nation, even over against the masses of the people and in the very circle of His disciples! In this narrowest circle He is to find His betrayer; and in the man to whom He says "Thou art the Rock . . . ," the man who denies Him thrice. And finally, it is the disciples of whom it is said that "they all forsook Him". And the people cry in chorus, "Away with him! Crucify him". The entire life of Jesus is lived in this loneliness and thus already in the shadow of the Cross.[11]

The shocking mystery of the gospel is that we are saved because Jesus suffered. "It is fitting that God," the writer of Hebrews continues, "should make

---

10. Irenaeus, *Against Heresies* II.22.4; in *ANF* 1: 391.
11. Barth, *Dogmatics in Outline*, 102–3.

the author of their salvation perfect through suffering" (2:10). In the same way that "he progressively opened himself to the mystery of God"—even in obedient suffering—we too have been given the capacity to open ourselves to God.[12] By identifying with humanity in the totality of our experience, even in being tempted just as we are (Heb 4:15), Jesus saves us by standing alongside us in our weakness.

Baptismal Grace

The baptism of Jesus is the beginning of his public ministry. However, there is much more about this event at the Jordan River. If John the Baptist preached "a baptism of repentance for the forgiveness of sins" (Mark 1:4), why would the sinless one be baptized? Moreover, why did Jesus say that his baptism must happen because "it is proper for us *in this way* to fulfill all righteousness" (Matt 3:15, italics mine)? Donald A. Hagner rightly points out that in his baptism, "Jesus thereby shows his solidarity with his people in their need. The Messiah is a representative person, the embodiment of Israel, whether as King or righteous Servant."[13] More pointedly, his baptism is his righteous act of identifying himself with sinners, lining up among those who are in need of baptism of repentance. Jesus' baptism points to his willingness to assume the sins of the world upon himself. We often recognize this on the cross (2 Cor 5:21; Matt 27:46), but his baptism also reveals it. If baptism is necessary for the forgiveness of sins, he fulfills all righteousness by being baptized on behalf of a world of sinners. He represents humanity in repentance. This is less dramatic than the cross, where he suffers and dies for us, but his saving work is the same. His water baptism and baptism of death (Luke 12:50) accomplish the same thing: the forgiveness of sins.

Moreover, it must be noted that upon being baptized, the Holy Spirit descended on Jesus and the Father spoke, "This is my Son, whom I love; with him I am well pleased" (Matt 3:16–17). These two important phenomena are also vicarious and exemplary in nature. Jesus is already conceived by the Spirit and is the Son of the Father. By engaging in repentance that leads to forgiveness, humanity may receive the Holy Spirit and become children of the Father. What is his becomes ours by grace. It is here that the great commissions in the four Gospels intersect. The command to baptize

12. Johnson, "Hebrews' Challenge to Christians," 21.
13. Hagner, *Matthew 1–13*, 56.

Grace and Salvation

(Matt 28:19) means that our role as disciples is to preach the good news of repentance (Mark 16:15; Luke 24:47) that leads to forgiveness (John 20:23). "Whoever believes and is baptized will be saved" (Mark 15:16). Willing hearers too will receive the Spirit of adoption (Rom 8:15–17) and become children of God (John 1:12). Jesus' baptism reveals the pre-requisite of salvation (i.e., repentance for the forgiveness of sins) and the consequence of salvation (i.e., becoming children of God and receiving the Holy Spirit).

He Did Not Sin

Immediately after his baptism, Jesus was led by the Spirit to be tempted in the wilderness (Matt 4:1). In his baptism he submitted to the righteous judgment of God against sin and identified with us, while in his temptation he opposed the power of evil and sin and triumphed over them for us. This is where we see the importance of the holiness of Jesus Christ in his saving work. As Thomas F. Torrance writes, "By his very holiness and perfect obedience sin had no power over him, and it was therefore as the holy one in entire fulfillment of the holy will of God that he invaded the domain of evil and redeemed us out of the power of darkness."[14] That "he was tempted in every way, yet he did not sin" (Heb 4:15) is not merely a statement of fact. It is related to his saving work. The paradoxical tension between Jesus becoming sin for us in his baptism and his holiness for us in his temptation, must be maintained.

Although Paul writes that the cross decisively dealt with usurping power (Col 2:15), Jesus' temptation inaugurated his conquest of these false authorities. Jesus' saving work deals with evil, temptation, and sin. His public ministry included many exorcisms. In the Gospel of Luke, Jesus' first recorded miracle was precisely to drive out an evil spirit from a man in Capernaum (Luke 4:31–35). This reveals the centrality of God's act on our behalf to liberate us from oppressive bondage. We see this foretold in the promise of God to crush the serpent's head through the seed of the woman (Gen 3:15) and foreshadowed in the destruction of Egypt to deliver the Israelites. In the temptation narrative, two things must be noted. First, he was full of the Spirit and was led by the Spirit to the wilderness (Luke 4:1). It is intriguing to think that the Spirit himself led Jesus to a place of temptation. Rather than understanding this as Jesus' passive obedience to the Spirit's leading, it must be perceived as Jesus' active act of invading Satan's

---

14. Torrance, *Atonement*, 32.

lair to wage war against him. Jesus comes to the wilderness as a warrior to defeat evil. He takes the initiative to invade the gates of hell and shows us how powerless evil can be even in his extreme physical weakness. He succeeds as one "full of the Spirit." What Jesus did is important, not only because we are powerless to overcome evil on our own, but also because the possibility of living victoriously as children of God requires two things: (1) the subjugation of evil powers that may continue to threaten us; and (2) our enablement through the Holy Spirit to overcome evil.

Saving Death of the Messiah

Admittedly, the New Testament devotes considerable attention to the saving death of Jesus. Most of our prominent models of atonement are based on it. This chapter will not elaborate these to avoid duplicating numerous available writings.[15] What will be emphasized here is Christ's saving work in the cross in continuity with his atoning life which began in the virgin birth. There are distinct salvific themes in the other aspects of Christ's life, but these that already emerged in the previous discussions—of substitution and representation, One for the many, vicarious atoning life, victory over evil—find their greatest expression in Jesus' death.

John Wesley stood in line with the Reformation emphasis on the substitutionary nature of Christ's death. Christ died for us and on our behalf. In recent years, this has been subjected to criticism because of its implications related to paternal violence and passive righteousness (i.e., the righteousness of Jesus is the sufficient substitute for believers' growth in holiness).[16] But the baby must not be thrown with the bath water. The concept of substitution goes back to Genesis 3:21, when an animal's life was taken to cover humanity's shame. Without the shedding of blood, there is no forgiveness of sins (Heb 9:22; Lev 16:16). The Old Testament temple sacrifices foreshadow Christ's death. In the words of Caiaphas, "it is better for [us] that one man die for the people than that the whole nation perish" (John 11:50).

---

15. For instance, Mozley, *The Doctrine of Atonement*; Banks, *Reconciliation and Hope*; Holmes, *The Wondrous Cross*; Vail, *Atonement and Salvation*, especially chapters 7–9.

16. Wood, "Suffering with the Crucified Christ," 185, 189. See also Collins, *The Theology of John Wesley*, 100–108, for a lengthier explanation. There are disagreements within Evangelicals about many things but there is consensus about two important things: we are lost as humans and that the cross is a climactic redemptive event. See Carson, "Reflections on Salvation," 592–93.

Grace and Salvation

The sacrificial and substitutionary death of Jesus happened "in accordance with the Scriptures" (1 Cor 15:3). Wright spends considerable effort to explain what this means in *The Day the Revolution Began*. Christ's death is not the just demand of a wrathful God to appease his anger, restore his honor, or do justice to his righteousness. Instead, it must be understood in the light of the history of Israel and its need for a suffering servant to take upon himself the fate of the nation. "At the center of the whole picture we do not find a wrathful God bent on killing someone, demanding blood," Wright says, "instead, we find the image . . . of the covenant-keeping God who takes the full force of sin unto himself."[17] Because the Messiah died for sinners who are incapable of restoring their relationship with God, the death of Jesus Christ reveals "the logic of hope" and "the logic of love."[18] This is crucial. We need to see the saving life and death of Jesus in continuity with God's grace in initiating relationships and sustaining his covenant. "The point about the Messiah's death, then, is that it demonstrates God's faithfulness to the covenant plan—the plan to rescue the whole world through Israel."[19] Jesus' self-sacrifice fulfills both covenant punishments and blessings.

Why is the death of Christ a "vocational necessity?"[20] What does it accomplish for us? This will be answered more extensively in the next chapter which deals with the "spiritual blessings" of being in Christ (Eph 1:3–14). Suffice it to say for now, following Wright, and in line with this book's previous chapter, that Christ's death dealt with the perennial issue of sin. If exile—theologically understood as our separation from God because of sin—is the universal problem, then God's radical and gracious solution is forgiveness wrought for us by Jesus standing in our place and on our behalf on the cross. The grace of the Lord Jesus Christ is his act of taking what should be ours and giving us forgiveness in return. God's love is this: "While we were still sinners, Christ died for us" (Rom 5:8). The consequence for us is a new Passover and a new Exodus, where humans are delivered from bondage and death, are set free to worship God, and are empowered to fulfill our lost vocation as royal priests.[21] God's rescue operation has at its core the sacrificial death of his incarnate Son to forgive our

---

17. Wright, *The Day the Revolution Began*, 185.
18. Wright, *The Day the Revolution Began*, 272.
19. Wright, *The Day the Revolution Began*, 320.
20. Wright, *The Day the Revolution Began*, 140.
21. Wright, *The Day the Revolution Began*, 324. See also Vail, *Atonement and Salvation*, chapter 6.

sins and restore us as humans created in his image. This, for Wright, is "the heart of the revolution that was launched on Good Friday" and "the power of self-giving love." [22] He took upon himself the sins of the world and bore its heavy weight, thereby experiencing humanity's alienation from God. His cry of dereliction at the cross, "My God, why have you forsaken me?" (Matt 27:46) is his prayer on our behalf, expressing humanity's deepest anxiety about the consequence of sin: our separation from God.

What Jesus did on the cross was something humans do not want to do: admit or confess our sins. When Adam and Eve sinned against God, they blamed each other instead of admitting their own faults (Gen 3:11–13). This is precisely where humanity fails: in refusing to believe that we are sinners. But this is what Jesus did on the cross. As the sinless one, he took upon himself humanity's sin and represented all of humanity before God, confessing, as it were, on our behalf. Moreover, at the cross, he accepted the punishment for sin. Adam and Eve did not admit their sin because they wanted to evade the consequence of their disobedience. This is what we, human beings, are also prone to do. But Jesus Christ did this at the cross. He not only confessed on behalf of all humanity; he also accepted the righteous judgment of God against sin. The cross is Jesus' "Amen" to God's holiness and justice.

The saving effect of Christ's self-less love is the creation of new humanity. "Somehow," Tom Noble writes, "the death of Christ *was* the death of sin—the expiation, the obliteration, the crucifixion of the old sinful, Adamic humanity."[23] We cannot achieve this on our own. Only God can accomplish this for us. Noble adds that at the cross,

> as our representative, he finally and fully denied that he had human rights to life, to liberty, and to the pursuit of happiness. He recognized that before God sinful humanity could claim no rights, and so, embodying humanity in his own Person, he claimed none: no right to the pursuit of happiness, for he gave himself to sorrow; no right to liberty, for he gave himself into captivity; no right to life, for he gave himself up to death. He was tempted to live for himself, for he was tempted on all points as we are (Heb 4:15). But there at the cross, the temptation to live according to the old Adamic self-interest, which he had denied and mortified within

---

22. Wright, *The Day the Revolution Began*, 222.
23. Noble, *Holy Trinity: Holy People*, 178.

Grace and Salvation

himself consistently and perfectly in his obedience to the Father at every moment of his life, finally and definitely died.[24]

Christ's selflessness, as our representative, undoes the power of sin that we have inherited from the first Adam. The challenge for us now, as followers of Jesus Christ, is to appropriate the same selflessness in our lives through the enabling power of the Holy Spirit. We will discuss this more in chapter 9.

The drama at the cross is the most vivid depiction of humanity's hatred toward God and God's self-less love toward humanity. The cross represents the whole of creation's hostile attitude toward its Creator. The stick that flogged his body, the stones that were thrown at him, the thorns that pricked his brow, the wood to which he was nailed—all of these are his creation inflicting pain on him. The creation that he fashioned with his own hands, the creatures that bear his image, the men and women to whom he bestowed intelligence and understanding, the souls to whom he awarded conscience, the strengths he provided for doing good works—all of these were used by his creation to murder him. The death of Jesus Christ at the cross is the tragic portrayal of the alienation between God and creation. But it is in this extremely hostile setting that God in Christ also displays his compassionate, self-giving love.

Raised with Christ the King

For Wright, the cross is the beginning of the revolution. But the resurrection is "the first visible sign that the revolution was already under way."[25] If in the cross Jesus embodied in himself our sin and punishment, in the resurrection he equally embodied our triumph over sin and death. The resurrection is the evidence that forgiveness of sins has been truly accomplished for us. If Jesus remained dead, we may only affirm the righteous judgment of God against sin. But because he is risen, we have confidence that God has received Christ's selfless sacrifice and vindicated him. Paul was very clear about this: "If Christ has not been raised, your faith is futile; you are still in your sins" and "we are of all people most to be pitied" (1 Cor 15:17–19). The resurrection is forgiveness actualized. In the story of the paralytic man in Mark 2:1–12, Jesus does not only utter "Your sins are forgiven," but also

---

24. Noble, *Holy Trinity: Holy People*, 178.
25. Wright, *The Day the Revolution Began*, 4.

says "Get up (Greek *egeiro*, "to rise"), take your mat and go home." Resurrection is the evidence of true forgiveness.

In Christ's resurrection God decisively dealt with the power of death. We now have confidence that death is not the final word. We can taunt with Paul: "Where, O death, is your victory? Where, O death, is your sting?" (1 Cor 15:55). If, according to Paul, "the last enemy to be destroyed is death" (1 Cor 15:26), then Christ effectively showed in his resurrection that death is already defeated. His resurrection "has destroyed all dominion, authority and power" that enslave and oppress humanity (1 Cor 15:24). This has radical implications for us. As the new Adam, Jesus is the "firstborn from among the dead" (Col 1:18) and "the firstfruit of those who have fallen asleep" (1 Cor 15:20). As his brothers and sisters, humanity too will be raised. Paul wrote: "If we have been united with him in a death like his, we will certainly also be united with him in a resurrection like his . . . if we died with Christ, we believe that we will also live with him" (Rom 6:5, 8). Indeed, "Thanks be to God! He gives us the victory through our Lord Jesus Christ" (1 Cor 15:57). Just as we have no more reason to fear death, we have no more reason to fear even the world itself. As Torrance wrote:

> The Christian Church that believes in the resurrection of Jesus Christ from the dead has no right to despair of "this weary world" or to be afraid it will crumble away into nothing. Christ is risen! He is completely victorious over the mighty demonic forces of destruction that threaten our world. In him we can lift up our heads and laugh in the face of disaster and death, for in him we are more than conquerors over all, knowing that God who raised Jesus from the dead, wearing our humanity, will not suffer the world for which he died and rose again to see corruption.[26]

The resurrection reveals God's power to give life. Just as he bestows life to a lump of dust (Gen 2:7) and to scattered bones (Ezek 37:1–14), God has the power to resurrect humanity from the dead (Acts 24:15; John 5:28). Just as the Spirit raised Jesus from the dead (1 Pet 3:18), we too may experience the work of "the life-giving Spirit" (1 Cor 15:45). There is more. The resurrection of Jesus reveals our future bodily resurrection or the redemption of our physicality. Our hope is not a salvation characterized by an escape of the formless soul to live in heaven, but an incorruptible body in the new heaven and new earth (1 Cor 15:42–44, 51–54). God's concern for the body is portrayed in Christ's healing miracles and even in raising people from

---

26. Torrance, *Karl Barth*, 23.

Grace and Salvation

the dead, but Christ's resurrection confirms that salvation involves freedom from bodily corruption and decay.

Interceding High Priest

Whereas the Protestant and Evangelical traditions emphasize the crucifixion of Christ, Maddox says that the Greek Orthodox tradition puts more emphasis on the resurrection and ascension.[27] Yes, the ascension is part of Christ's saving work, particularly his priestly ministry: "Who then is the one who condemns? No one. Christ Jesus who died—more than that, who was raised to life—is at the right hand of God and is also interceding for us" (Rom 8:34). Christ's saving mediation extends through the ascension. He acts as our advocate before the Father. "The purpose of ascension," Oden writes, "is intercession."[28] I imagine his prayer right now to be similar to his utterance on the cross: "Father, forgive them for they do not know what they are doing" (Luke 23:34). Understanding our human way of life and thinking, he is the "merciful and faithful high priest" who is able to empathize with our weaknesses (Heb 2:17; 4:15). He is able to pray this because he lived as a human and was "tempted like us in every way."[29] His solidary with us as humans is entirely in our favor.

The letter to the Hebrews points to the high priestly role of Jesus Christ in our salvation. Jesus is the "high priest forever" (7:2). He is in "the order of Melchizedek" because he is the king of righteousness and peace. Jesus serves at the throne of God "bringing many sons to glory" (2:10). His priestly role must also be understood in the light of God's covenant faithfulness. Although provision was given in the old covenant for the forgiveness of sins through the blood of a victim (Lev 16:16; Heb 9:22), these sacrifices were never the solution to the problem of sin and covenant breaking. Jesus' priestly work, however, deals with this permanently. But how, and does this mean that the shedding of his blood at Calvary is insufficient? The ascended priest's saving work is not about sufficiency or insufficiency; it is about the nature of his work. Richard D. Nelson explains the importance of the ascension by alluding to the Day of Atonement in Leviticus 16, which is divided into three parts: (1) the death of the victim, (2) the passage of the

27. Maddox, *Responsible Grace*, 96.

28. Oden, *John Wesley's Scripture Way of Salvation*, 183. See also Maddox, *Responsible Grace*, 110.

29. See also Eugenio, "Following Jesus the Reconciler," 103–6.

priest into the Holy of Holies, and (3) the use of blood to effect purification and to renew covenantal relationship.[30] N. T Wright is correct: "the death of the sacrificial animal was not the heart of the ritual; it was only the preliminary event. What mattered was that the blood . . . would then be presented on the altar."[31] Christ's entry to and presence at the right hand of the Father are aspects of his saving work. Of course this does not mean that the death and resurrection of Christ are ineffective, so Jesus must intercede for us. It means that Christ's saving work is continuous. Jesus saved us, is saving us, and will save us. There is no day in our lives in which we no longer need the atoning work of Jesus Christ. We depend on him for our salvation through and through.

Conclusions

This chapter presented the saving life of Christ, from his birth to his continuing work as the ascended high priest. We highlighted the fact that "the grace of the Lord Jesus Christ" is embodied throughout his life. Our salvation is through him in the entirety of his life and work. Everything that happened to him is for us. The events before and after the cross are not second-rate preludes and postludes, but are essential parts of his saving mission as the incarnate Son. Knowing this, we develop a profound appreciation of Jesus' entire life and a deeper understanding of the nature of salvation. It must be noted, however, that this chapter deals primarily with what Jesus Christ does for us. In theological jargon, we only discussed the objective work of Christ. This is intentional, because an elaboration concerning our participation or co-operation with God's saving grace will be done in chapter 9. Wesleyan theology offers resources and reasons for this, particularly when we consider the work of the Holy Spirit. Moreover, in this chapter, we have dealt only with the nature of Christ's saving work; we have yet to discuss the nature of the salvation that he has accomplished for us. This also requires lengthy discussion. So we turn to that topic in the next chapter.

---

30. Nelson, "'He Offered Himself," 251–65.
31. Wright, *The Day the Revolution Began*, 177.

8

Salvific Gifts

"Praise be to the God and Father of our Lord Jesus Christ, who has blessed us in the heavenly realms with every spiritual blessing in Christ"

—EPHESIANS 1:3

"All the blessings which God hath bestowed upon man," John Wesley noted, "are of his mere grace, bounty, or favour: his free, undeserved favour, favour altogether undeserved, man having no claim to the least of his mercies."[1] We have received "the riches of God's grace that he lavished on us" (Eph 1:7–8). The good news of salvation is that plenty of gifts await those who believe in the Lord Jesus Christ. Salvation involves addition. When we are born again, God transforms our existence from spiritual destitution to opulence. These gifts are concretely felt and existentially experienced here and now. In this chapter, we will understand our new situation as Christians, which will lead us to have a serious appreciation of what God does for and in us and to develop a deeper sense of worshipful gratitude to our gracious God. Realizing the depth of divine magnanimity also elicits us to contemplate on our responsibility as recipients of his grace.

---

1. Wesley, "Salvation by Faith," in *Works* (BE) 1: 117.

Salvific Gifts

What is Salvation?

Salvation—and receiving its benefits—is a present and future reality. Salvation is not an escape of the soul from the body to a realm outside of current life. This Platonized version of salvation—elevating the soul and diminishing the body—that plagues much of Christianity produces Christians whose vision is limited to the future. This in turn can result in passivity and conscious neglect of our priestly vocation in the world today. In contrast, N. T. Wright asserts: "The New Testament insists, in book after book, that when Jesus of Nazareth died on the cross, something happened as a result of which the world is a different place . . . The New Testament, with the story of Jesus' crucifixion at the center, is about God's kingdom coming on earth as it is in heaven."[2] The Christian hope is that God transforms our existence here and now. Indeed, "now is the day of salvation" (2 Cor 6:2). Our denominational emphasis on the sanctified life expresses the Wesleyan affirmation of the present quality of salvation. This does not come as a surprise, because Wesley himself underscored this. In his sermon "The Scripture Way of Salvation," he argued that salvation makes a difference now. Salvation is "not what is frequently understood by that word, the going to heaven, eternal happiness," he wrote. "It is not a blessing which lies on the other side of death . . . it is a present thing, a blessing which, through the free mercy of God, ye are now in possession of."[3] Salvation is an unending journey of grace and of being constantly sanctified through and through (1 Thess 5:23). Although it is true that our full salvation awaits consummation in Jesus' second coming, we are already saved (aorist terms used in Eph 2:5-6) and are also continuously being "transformed into his image with ever-increasing glory" (2 Cor 3:18).

And because salvation is "not rescue *from* the present world, but rescue and renewal *within* the present world,"[4] it is communal, cosmic, and missional. The purpose of salvation is not a reception of this and that gift for individual enjoyment. Rather, it is "to enable people to become fully functioning, fully image-bearing human beings within God's world, already now."[5] This is the revolutionary aspect of Christ's saving work. The kingdom of God is at work in our midst, affecting the lives of people

---

2. Wright, *The Day the Revolution Began*, 39–40.
3. Wesley, "The Scripture Way of Salvation," in *Works* (BE) 2: 156.
4. Wright, *The Day the Revolution Began*, 113.
5. Wright, *The Day the Revolution Began*, 155.

and permeating society. Because salvation is also therapeutic in nature, its healing effect is felt now in the restoration of life, recovery of the image of God, and renewal of our whole being. That this can happen now, and in an instant, has pastoral, evangelical, and missional significance. Wesley discerned: "Our word does not profit, either as to justification or sanctification, unless we can bring them to expect the blessing while we speak."[6] So what happens when we are born again, converted, made new creatures in Christ by the Holy Spirit? What spiritual blessings do we receive? What happens to us here and now?

Forgiveness of Sins

It is sin that creates enmity between God and humanity, so forgiveness of sins is the gracious act of God in restoring humanity to intimate relationship with him. The death of Christ provides justification for us (1 Cor 15:3). Through his blood, God overlooks our sins and proclaims us righteous. He acquits us and frees us from the just punishment that is due for us. Because of Jesus, our advocate and high priest, God no longer considers our past. We are released from guilt and shame. We begin to enjoy true peace with God because we receive "salvation from sin and the consequence of sin" and "deliverance from guilt and punishment."[7]

Justification does not mean that the sins of the past are undone, or that their physical, natural, and social consequences magically disappear. Neither does it mean that the reality of our past sins becomes untruth, as if they did not happen at all. The facts of past history do not change as a result of Christ's work. Forgiveness means that God no longer takes our past sins into consideration in our relationship with him.[8] He forgives our sins so that our present and future are no longer tied to what we have done; everything now hinges on what Christ has done for us. Here, it must be underscored that it is only our past sins that are forgiven. The Reformation emphasis on justification by faith must not be stretched to mean that future sins are

---

6. Wesley, *Letters* 5: 316; quoted in Collins, *The Theology of John Wesley*, 186.

7. Wesley, "Salvation by Faith," in *Works* (BE) 1: 124.

8. Jan Muis writes: "God is just in justification in that he re-establishes and creates a just relation or just order between himself and men by maintaining his worth and right, by pronouncing and executing his judgment on human injustice, and by giving men the right to be his creatures, covenant-partners, and children," in "Justification and the Justice of God," 186–87.

negligible, to be ignored, because of a lifetime guarantee of pardon we once received. The proposal that all our sins—past, present, and future—are unconditionally forgiven already may result in Christian life characterized by "insurance *for* sin rather than freedom *from* its guilt."[9] This is contrary to biblical expectations of a transformed and holy life. God's pardoning grace must not serve as a license to sin. Instead, it must enkindle a heart full of gratitude to God's grace that compels us to live in righteousness.

Additionally, justification does not mean that God deceives himself or us. The argument in some traditions that our sins are merely covered by the blood of Christ so that he no longer sees our unchanged real nature, implies that God does not actually deal with the problem of sin. Supposedly sin remains, albeit hidden from God's sight. The blood of Jesus that covers us blinds the Father from seeing true reality or deceives the Father so that he unknowingly (or ignorantly) absolves us of our sins. This cannot be. The grace of God in Christ is that he justifies us in his full awareness that we are sinners. Nothing is hidden from God. We must highlight that real forgiveness involves cleansing from sin (1 John 1:9). King David's prayer was for a cleansing of his iniquities that results in becoming whiter than snow, having a pure heart, and being restored in the joy of salvation (Ps 51:2, 7, 10–12). Justification is "not a legal fiction. It effects real change in a person's heart, soul, mind, and relationships."[10]

Reconciled with God

The immediate consequence of sin is broken relationships. When we steal a friend's property or do violence against someone, our offense creates animosity, a breach of trust that causes separation. The same is true in divine-human relationships: "Your iniquities have separated you from your God; your sins have hidden his face from you" (Isa 59:2). However, because our sins are forgiven, we experience restored relationship and peace with God. Christianity is not primarily a religion of activity, allegiance to a particular denomination, or affirmation of a set of beliefs. It is about being restored to right relationship with God. We were once "alienated from God and were enemies" (Col 1:21), but "while we were God's enemies, we were reconciled to him through the death of his Son" (Rom 5:10). There was a time when we "were separate from Christ, excluded from citizenship in

---

9. Collins, *The Theology of John Wesley*, 173.
10. Burroughs, "Wesley's Presentation of Salvation," 207.

Israel and foreigners to the covenants of the promise, without hope and without God in the world. But now in Christ Jesus [we] who once were far away have been brought near by the blood of Christ" (Eph 2:12–13). Paul's presentation of the contrast before and after reconciliation is dramatic and decisive. The change is truly radical. The transition is from alienation to intimacy with God.

Reconciliation is important because it nullifies the wages of sin: spiritual death and alienation (Rom 6:23). In chapter 2, we observed that sin causes at least three broken relationships: human alienation from God, social fragmentation, and human abuse of creation. By the blood of Jesus Christ, peace and reconciliation are possible in all three aspects (Col 1:20). First, we are restored to God's favor because God no longer counts our sins against us (2 Cor 5:19). Second, as forgiven people, we are also called to forgive and be reconciled to others (John 20:23; Col 2:13; Matt 5:23–24). In fact, we have been entrusted the ministry of reconciliation (2 Cor 5:19–20). Our reconciliation with God must lead to our becoming communion-constituting people, living out the reconciled life in social relationships (Mark 9:50; Rom 12:8; 14:19; 2 Cor 13:11; 1 Thess 5:13; Heb 12:14; Jas 3:18). Jesus proclaimed, "blessed are the peacemakers" (Matt 5:9). "The attitude of forgiveness," James Earl Massey writes, "motivates one to set aside that which causes distance, and the spirit of inclusiveness exhibits openness by which togetherness can begin and achieve development."[11] Third, as forgiven people, we ought to rediscover our vocation as stewards of creation (Gen 1:28). All violence toward the environment should cease, to be replaced by intentional care.

God's gift of reconciliation must not come as a surprise. In the creation narrative in Genesis, God is already portrayed as inviting, fellowship-constituting, and relational; he initiates relationship. God's gracious ability to forgive repentant people and remain faithful in his covenant with Israel reveal his reconciling nature. Reconciliation is possible, in addition to God's gracious magnanimity, because God sees worth in humans. Massey is correct: reconciliation "requires a focus on the other person as someone of value."[12] For God, created reality is a treasured possession worth redeeming at the cost of his Son's life.

---

11. Massey, "Reconciliation," 14.
12. Massey, "Reconciliation," 14.

Salvific Gifts

New Birth, New Creation, and New Life

"If anyone is in Christ," Paul writes, "he is a new creation. The old has gone, the new has come" (2 Cor 5:17). Salvation has retrospective and prospective elements. Not only are our sins forgiven, which deals with our past; our present is also transformed by the gifts of reconciliation and new birth. Forgiveness and reconciliation change our relationship with God, creating intimacy. But new birth also changes our whole existence and identity. The latter is important because God's concern includes a believer's present and future life. We are saved toward a life of obedience to the divine will, and transformation is a pre-requisite for fulfilling this. We cannot live in the Spirit unless we are "born again" or "born of the Spirit" (John 3:3, 5). Forgiveness deals with past guilt and shame; new birth enables the believer to live in obedient life that results in continuous freedom from guilt and shame.

The debate surrounding imputed and imparted righteousness must not lead us to regard them as mutually exclusive. Wesley's understanding of faith is helpful in providing the balance between these two concepts. W. Stephen Gunter explains:

> Believers receive by faith the righteousness of Christ imputed to them, but the active faith of believers also results in the righteousness of Christ being "*implanted* in everyone to whom he has *imputed* it." The active and passive obedience of Christ are together the *sole meritorious cause* of our justification, and the result is both an imputed (passive) and imparted (active) righteousness in us. Justification is still by faith, but faith is more than rational assent. Faith is participation in the divine reality, the very righteousness of Christ.[13]

Justification is God's work through and through. No human merit may be presented to God in exchange for the forgiveness of our sins. However, although forgiveness is God's work *for* us, the new birth is God's work *in* us. Forgiveness involves change in relation with God, while regeneration involves real change in us. God does something for us so that we are not trapped in the misery of our old self characterized by disobedience. God does not declare us righteous while leaving our fallen nature untouched; he makes us righteous by transforming us. Wesleyan theologian Kenneth Collins presents a helpful table of comparison:[14]

---

13. Gunter, *The Limits of Love Divine*, 274.
14. Collins, *The Theology of John Wesley*, 201.

Justification	Regeneration
implies a relative change	implies a real change
God does something "for us"	God does something "in us"
changes our outward relation to God	changes our inmost souls so that we become saints
restores us to favor with God	restores us to the image of God
takes away the guilt of sin	takes away the power of sin

Collins further explains their difference by asserting that new birth is a necessary change, a vast change, a crucial change, and a liberating change.[15] First, the new birth is a necessary change because of the corruption of our human nature. Unless our fallen nature is healed and transformed, we will continuously live in sin, along with hopelessness, guilt, and shame. The human problem is not merely external; it is internal. Hence, the solution in inward change. Second, the new birth is also a vast change because it is a complete work that affects the whole human self. Our disposition, will, and way of thinking are all changed toward a life that pleases God. Third, the new birth is a crucial change that happens miraculously and instantaneously, although it may be preceded by periods of examination, conviction, or sorrow. It is not a gradual intellectual affirmation of the tenets of faith, a steady progress to moral living, or the consequence of either. Rather, it marks the beginning "of a qualitative change that issues in a distinct kind of life, a life that men and women cannot bring about by themselves."[16] Finally, the new birth is a liberating change because it frees us from the power of sin, both outward and inward. Regeneration is God's mighty, empowering act so that believers may overcome temptations.

The new birth is the beginning of the life that God plans for us. It is the humanization of humanity. "The new birth," Oden writes, "brings into being not only a new life, but a new will, and a new beginning for the redeemed affections. A new spiritual nature is being offered . . . so that one is born again into a new capacity to mirror the original image of God in humanity."[17] Our capacity to make good choices toward obedience to

---

15. Collins, *The Theology of John Wesley*, 205–22.
16. Collins, *The Theology of John Wesley*, 213.
17. Oden, *John Wesley's Scriptural Christianity*, 296.

God's will is restored, our ability to relate with others in camaraderie and our vocation to be stewards of creation are reactivated, and our calling to reflect God's righteousness and holiness is returned to its proper course. Regeneration "allows these earthen vessels to yield so as to reflect anew the love, power, and goodness of God. This new life is quickened by faith made active in love."[18] These are also made possible because in being born again, our spiritual senses are opened and attuned to God in an unprecedented manner. This is the work of the Holy Spirit.

Adopted as Children of God

"You are no longer foreigners and strangers," Paul writes, "but fellow citizens with God's people and also members of his household" (Eph 2:19). Forgiveness of sin results not only in reconciliation with God as friends; it entails the bestowal of the privilege to become children of God (John 1:12). Because we are born again and are baptized in the name of the Father, Son, and Holy Spirit, we now belong to God's family. Adoption and reconciliation highlight the change in our relationship with God, but adoption underscores a higher order in the divine-human relationship. The change that happens in our standing before God is radical: "You are no longer a slave, but God's child; and since you are his child, God has made you also an heir" (Gal 4:7). From being objects of God's wrath because of sin, we become recipients of his inheritance (Rom 8:17).

Our adoption as children of God reveals the magnanimity of God's grace. John wonders at this truth: "See what great love the Father has lavished on us, that we should be called children of God!" (1 John 3:1). John is astonished because he is aware of the prior alienation caused by sin and its resulting corruption. Thomas Watson states this succinctly: "We have enough in us to move God to correct us, but nothing to move him to adopt us."[19] But in his grace, God bestows the gift of participation in his family. Unlike human family planning designed to restrict size, God's family is ever expanding, incorporating, and welcoming. When John expressed our adoption into the family of God, he had in mind the practice of Roman society, in which a person (usually an adolescent, not an infant) who is not related to a family may become an heir to the family's inheritance. Adoption, thus, is solely by grace. We were not unknown to God. In fact we were

---

18. Oden, *John Wesley's Scriptural Christianity*, 296.
19. Watson, *A Body of Practical Divinity*, 160.

Grace and Salvation

formerly enemies harboring hostility towards him (Eph 2:14, 16). In his mercy, he has chosen us to become heirs of his riches.[20]

We become children of God not by nature, but by adoption. Only Jesus Christ is the Son of God by nature. This means that we join the family of God not as deified beings, but as humans in our creaturely nature and limitation. When the Apostle Peter wrote that we become "partakers of the divine nature" (2 Pet 1:4), he meant that by grace we now share in his holiness and love. He did not mean a transformation to divinity. Plato's use of the phrase in his book *Phaedrus* may shed light about what Peter means. Phaedrus asked Socrates if he heard about the myth of the Huntress in Boreas. Socrates responded that he had no time for such myths. Rather, he should give his time "to the study not of fables, but of my own self, that I may see whether I am really a more complicated and a more furious monster than Typhon, or a creature of a gentler and a simpler sort, the born *heir of a divine and tranquil nature.*"[21] Plato thought that a person either possesses a beastly character or a godly gentleness. Participating then in the nature of God implies possessing "godliness" (2 Pet 1:3). We have "adoption to sonship" so that we might be "conformed to the image of his Son" (Rom 8:23, 29).

This implies that in being adopted, we now bear God's name. This is reinforced by being baptized in the name of the Father, Son, and Holy Spirit. Our spiritual last name and relational identification are now found in God. This is a privilege with a great responsibility. In fact, we must avoid precisely where the Israelites failed when they defiled God's name among the nations (Exo 20:7; Lev 18:21; Amos 2:7; Mal 1:12). Our lives, our dealing with others, our decision-making, our actions, our words, our dispositions, our lifestyles, and everything that we do, must glorify the name of our Lord. This is the essence of the command of Jesus in Matthew 5:16: "Let your light shine before others, that they may see your good deeds and glorify your Father in heaven." By living holy lives as God's children, we reflect who he is in the world. This is not difficult to understand. Quite simply, if "we are God's handiwork, created in Christ Jesus to do good works" (Eph 2:10), but were to live not in accordance with the values of the divine household, then we would raise suspicions among nonbelievers about the God whose name we bear. Our position as God's children must produce childlike reverence and love for him.

---

20. Beeke, "Our Glorious Adoption," 63–79.
21. Plato, *Five Works of Plato*, 209.

Adoption is closely connected to assurance of salvation. The witness of the Spirit of adoption that we are children of God is central to the New Testament and for Wesleyan theology (Rom 8:14–16). In his sermon "Walking by Faith and not by Sight," Wesley asserted:

> How short is this description of real Christians! And yet how exceeding full! It comprehends, it sums up, the whole experience of those that are truly such, from the time they are born of God till they move into Abraham's bosom. For, who are the we that are here spoken of? All that are true Christian believers. I say Christian, not Jewish, believers. All that are not only servants, but children, of God. All that have "the Spirit of adoption, crying in their hearts, Abba, Father." All that have "the Spirit of God witnessing with their spirits, that they are the sons of God."[22]

The internal sign that we are indeed forgiven, reconciled, and regenerated is because the Holy Spirit testifies to us that we are God's children. Although Wesley increasingly preferred the term "evidence" over "assurance," his emphasis on the importance of conviction that one is born of God remained the same.[23] "The true, living Christian faith," he wrote, "which whoever hath 'is born of God', is not only . . . an act of the understanding, but a disposition which God hath wrought in his heart; a 'sure trust and confidence in God that through the merits of Christ his sins are forgiven, and he is reconciled to the favour of God.'"[24]

Sanctification

The comprehensiveness of our salvation is expressed beautifully by Paul: "You were washed, you were sanctified, you were justified in the name of the Lord Jesus Christ and by the Spirit of our God" (1 Cor 6:11). Two things merit consideration. First, being sanctified is God's gracious gift to us. As such, it is not something we work toward or achieve for ourselves. Relationally, our sanctification is related to being reconciled with God and adopted as his children. We have been called from darkness to light and are now set apart from the world to become God's treasured possession (Exo 19:5–6). Because God owns us, we become members of a holy nation. The grace of God is this: "Once you were not a people, but now you are the people of

---

22. Wesley, "Walking by Faith and not by Sight," in *Works* (BE) 4: 49.
23. Cherry, "Wesley's Doctrinal Distinctions," 107, 110.
24. Wesley, "The Marks of the New Birth," in *Works* (BE) 1: 418–19.

God" (1 Pet 2:9–10). Holiness is ultimately derivative. We are holy only because we are related to God.

However, positional or relational holiness must be accompanied by moral transformation. In new birth, the moral image of God in humanity is restored, thus enabling us to live holy lives. Although Wesley affirmed the imputation of righteousness, which he gained from the Moravians and the Reformed tradition, he also affirmed that "God implants righteousness in everyone to whom he has imputed it."[25] He was particularly wary of antinomianism, or that Christians would use positional holiness as a cloak that hides and legitimizes habitual unrighteousness. Biblical sanctification must involve real transformation in a person's life. So although we passively receive Christ's righteousness, we also begin to actively pursue righteousness in life through God's enabling grace in the Holy Spirit. "Do you not believe inherent righteousness?" Wesley asked, "Yes, in its proper place; not as the ground of our acceptance with God, but as the fruit of it; not in the place of imputed righteousness, but as consequent upon it."[26]

Being sanctified by God equips us to produce fruits "in keeping with repentance" (Matt 3:8). Righteousness is not an effort that merits God's favor. It is the other way around. Because God has shown us favor, in gratitude we live in righteousness. The paradoxical tension of "the Protestant ethic of grace with the Catholic ethic of holiness"[27] must be maintained. Of course, the priority of grace in our sanctification must be underscored in order to avoid accusations of works righteousness. However, the generosity of grace must not lead to wanton disregard of God's laws and requirement for obedience. "Sanctification is the work of God's free grace," Wesley wrote, "whereby we are renewed in the whole person after the image of God, and are enabled to die unto sin and live unto righteousness."[28]

When we are born again, we are set free from the power and bondage of sin, liberated from Satan's rule, and restored to God's lordship. We are not only freed *from* sin's dominion; we are also freed *for* God's reign. In particular, we become free to love. Oden writes: "In evangelical existence, one experiences oneself as free, not in a falsely fantasized liberty of moral sluggishness, but a true liberty to love the neighbor . . . also for the life of

---

25. Wesley, "The Lord Our Righteousness," in *Works* (BE) 1: 458.
26. Wesley, "The Lord Our Righteousness," in *Works* (BE) 1: 458.
27. Cell, *The Rediscovery of John Wesley*, 347.
28. Wesley, *The Works of John Wesley*, 12: 101–2; quoted in Collins and Johnson, "From the Garden to the Gallows," 22–23.

faith active in love."[29] Love is the foundation of all our pursuit of God and service to our fellow human beings. Wesley is worth quoting at length:

> In a Christian believer love sits upon the throne, which is erected in the inmost soul; namely love of God and man, which fills the whole heart, and reigns without a rival. In a circle near the throne are all holy tempers: long-suffering, gentleness, meekness, goodness, fidelity, temperance—and if any other is comprised in "the mind which was in Christ Jesus." In an exterior circle are all the works of mercy, whether to the souls or bodies of men. By these we exercise all holy tempers; by these we continually improve them, so that all these are real means of grace, although this is not commonly adverted to. Next to these are those that are usually termed works of piety: reading and hearing the Word, public, family, private prayer, receiving the Lord's Supper, fasting or abstinence. Lastly, that his followers may the more effectively provoke one another to love, holy tempers, and good works, our blessed Lord has united them together in one—the church—dispersed all over the earth; a little emblem of which, of the church universal, we have in every particular Christian congregation.[30]

Love compels us to worship God and to do good to others. A husband who dearly loves his wife will do everything to make her happy. A friend who truly loves his friend would not intentionally do anything to grieve him. Love enkindles our hearts to choose what pleases "the other" and prevents us from doing things that will break our relationship with them. This is why Wesley asserted that love of God and others are important marks of an "altogether Christian."[31]

Conclusions

Salvation is a gift with many accompanying gifts. It is not simply accepting Jesus Christ as our Lord and Savior. It entails receiving several spiritual blessings that we as humans will never achieve for ourselves. When we put our faith in the Lord Jesus Christ and repent from our sins, we are forgiven and are reconciled to God to be his friends and children. We are set

---

29. Oden, *John Wesley's Scriptural Christianity*, 285. The ideal is this: "love not only burning in your hearts, but flaming in all your actions and conversations, making your whole life one 'labor of love,'" in Runyon, "The New Creation," 17.

30. Wesley, "On Zeal," in *Works* (BE) 3: 313–14.

31. Wesley, "Almost Christian," in *Works* (BE) 1: 137–38.

free from sin's bondage and are redeemed to become God's possessions. We are also restored to the humanity we ought to be and have, and are "transformed into his image with ever-increasing glory" (2 Cor 3:18). But accompanying our reception of spiritual blessings is our responsibility to live out our new identity as God's holy people. As renewed creation, we are enabled to fulfil our original vocation to worship and serve the Lord in and for the world. Such enablement is crucial in our understanding of grace and salvation. As we shall see in the next chapter, this is the work of the Holy Spirit, who is active in our lives before, during, and after our conversion. Moreover, by looking at the work of the Holy Spirit, we will understand that God's grace is responsible grace.

9

Empowering Grace

> "For we were all baptized by one Spirit so as to form one body—whether Jews or Gentiles, slave or free—and we were all given the one Spirit to drink"
>
> —1 CORINTHIANS 12:13

OUR SALVATION IS THE work of the triune God, but there is a tendency among many Evangelical traditions to neglect both the Father and the Holy Spirit in our discussion of God's gracious saving work, primarily because of our Christ-centeredness. Much of the literature available highlights Christ's work. This approach leads to theological misunderstandings such as limited atonement and universalism because both only look at the saving work of Christ without considering the enabling work of the Holy Spirit. Emphasizing the work of the Holy Spirit shies us away from deterministic understandings of salvation. Although salvation is the work of God, he does not do so by irresistible divine fiat. Paradoxically, even though Christ died for all, not everyone will be saved. There are other variables to consider aside from Christ's work. For instance, what is the role of humans—possessing God-given freedom corrupted by sin—in all these? Wesleyans are in a better position to address questions related to human agency—whether in the form of acceptance or rejection of God's saving offer—because of our insistent affirmation of the work of the Spirit before, during, and after conversion. Moreover, this enables us to have a theologically balanced view of grace as an enablement that demands appropriate response.

The Spirit in Salvation

The work of the Holy Spirit is a key factor in every Christian experience. This of course includes our salvation. We are at home with this because Wesley's affirmation of the Holy Spirit is packed with soteriological overtones:

> I believe the infinite and eternal Spirit of God, equal with the Father and the Son, to be not only perfectly holy in himself but the immediate cause of all holiness in us; enlightening our understandings, renewing our natures, uniting our persons to Christ, assuring us of our adoption as sons, leading us in our actions, purifying and sanctifying our souls and bodies, to a full and central enjoyment of God.[1]

The generous presence and work of the Holy Spirit in us and for our salvation reveal that the Spirit is probably the most overworked Person of the Trinity. This is especially true when we think of grace not as an impersonal force, substance, or power that God dispenses to effect salvation. Grace is not a divine decree that implements change at a distance. Grace is not "a possession given to humanity to justify God's mercy," but is "the accompanying effect of the Divine energies present in our lives through the Holy Spirit."[2] Understood as divine presence, grace therefore is personal and relational. Where the Holy Spirit is, there grace is.

The Holy Spirit is active in the lives of people from birth to death, including those who continuously resist his convicting work. His specific office is to glorify the Son (John 16:14), to reveal Christ's atoning work, and to convict the world about sin, about their attitude towards Christ, and about judgment (John 16:8–11). Clearly, the saving work of the Spirit cannot be separated from the saving work of Christ. The Spirit makes the atoning work of Christ a present reality in the world, leading people to experience forgiveness of sins made available for us through and in Christ. This is why it is common nomenclature in Christian theology to refer to the Holy Spirit as "the Administrator of redemption."[3] The Spirit enables us to experience what Christ has done for us. In Reformed language, the

---

1. Wesley, *Works* (JE) 10: 82.
2. Maddox, *Responsible Grace*, 86.
3. Collins, *The Theology of John Wesley*, 122.

Holy Spirit subjectively applies to us today the objective work of Christ 2000 years ago. By bringing us to Christ, we experience pardon for our sins and become new creation in being born of the Spirit. Roger Hahn says it beautifully: "The Spirit takes the objective, external work of Christ and internalizes it in the believer. The Spirit makes the life of Christ real in the life of the believer."[4]

Maddox narrates five dimensions of the Spirit's saving work, which will form the basic outline of this chapter, with a bit of modification: (1) restoring work of the Spirit for all, (2) enablement of human freedom, (3) witness of the Spirit among believers, (4) fruit of the Spirit in sanctification, and (5) gifts of the Spirit for Christian service.[5] These dimensions reflect important Wesleyan emphases about the Spirit's involvement throughout a person's life up to progressive sanctification, and encompass Wesleyan spirituality that integrates works of piety with works of mercy.

Restoring Work of the Spirit

Scriptures affirm that humans are born in sin (Ps 51:5) and are incapable of choosing God. We are totally depraved. Our hearts are sick (Jer 17:9). Our inward disposition leads us to commit sin (Gen 6:5, 11; 8:21; Rom 7:5, 23) and satisfy the desires of the flesh (Gal 5:17). Sin affects our mind or reason (Rom 1:21; 2 Cor 3:14–15, 4:4) and our emotions or affections (Rom 1:26–27; Gal 5:24; 2 Tim 3:2–4). Our wills are also "slaves to sin" (Rom 6:17; 2 Tim 2:25–26). The question, therefore, is: as people under the power of sin (Rom 3:9), how do we get to the point where we actually choose God over our evil inclination? As Brian Edgar succinctly worded, "There are many things that individuals can do on their own, but being a Christian is not one of them."[6] So how does God save us from our abject predicament? Left on our own, we are doomed to damnation, so what does God do to save us in a way that is consistent with his nature as holy, loving, and just?

The response is provided by Paul: "For it is by grace you have been saved, through faith—and this is not from yourselves, it is the gift of God— not by works, so that no one can boast" (Eph 2:8–9). Various theological traditions have their unique interpretations of these verses. For Roman Catholics, grace is meritorious. We receive grace through the merits of our

4. Hahn, "Pneumatology in Romans 8," 86.
5. Maddox, *Responsible Grace*, 123.
6. Edgar, *The Message of the Trinity*, 290.

good works or through the treasury of merits that we can access through church-instituted means. For Calvinists, grace is unconditionally given to those who have been predestined for salvation. Because all of humanity are doomed and cannot save themselves, it is gracious that God chooses some—using an unknown selection criterion (if there is)—to be saved. For Calvinists, Jesus Christ died on the cross specifically for the elect. God's saving grace is irresistible; the chosen shall be saved. Moreover, no one can deny the chosen of their right to be saved, regardless of their lifestyle on earth. Not even angels or demons may snatch the chosen from the hand of God and cause them to lose their salvation.

Like the Calvinists, Wesleyans affirm that sinful humanity is incapable of choosing God on our own. Unlike Calvinists, however, Wesleyans argue that grace is free but does not operate by coercive fiat. Instead, grace enables us to choose God. We call it prevenient grace because it highlights the priority of divine action in the order of salvation for entities who are totally depraved. Prevenient grace is for all, regardless of gender or race. There is a sense, therefore, in which prevenient grace is irresistible, because God's work is not a matter of our own prerogative. Whether we like it or not, the Holy Spirit works in everyone. As Wesley asserted, "there is no man that is in a state of mere nature" or one who is "wholly devoid of the grace of God."[7] The fact that sinful humans have a certain measure of self-control so that they are not as sinful as they can possibly be is an evidence of conscience, which is the work of "preventing grace."[8]

The primary consequence of grace—as the work of the Holy Spirit—is the re-enablement of our corrupted human faculties that were meant to glorify God in the first place. Five specific benefits may be enumerated, which may be understood as God's work in partially mitigating the effects of the Fall in humanity. First, prevenient grace allows us to know basic knowledge of God, mostly related to his divine attributes. Paul wrote about this in Romans 1:19–20: "What may be known about God is plain to them, because God has made it plain to them. For since the creation of the world God's invisible qualities—his eternal power and divine nature—have been clearly seen, being understood from what has been made, so that people are without excuse." Second, prevenient grace gives human beings, in some measure, an awareness of the demands of God's moral law. For Wesley, God's "first step is to enlighten the understanding by that general knowledge of good

---

7. Wesley, "On Working Out Our Own Salvation," in *Works* (BE) 3: 207.
8. Wesley, "On Working Out Our Own Salvation," in *Works* (BE) 3: 207.

and evil. To this he adds many secret reproofs, if they act contrary to light."[9] This is related to the third benefit, which is the activity of conscience in sinful humanity that acts as God's "umpire . . . an inward judge, which passes sentence both on his passions and actions, either approving or condemning them."[10] Fourth, the Holy Spirit partially restores human will, so that we are enabled to respond positively to conscience and live out our basic knowledge of good and evil. Fifth, and as a result of the combination of the four mentioned benefits, prevenient grace restrains human wickedness, so that we do not sin in every way possible, as much as possible.[11]

Considering prevenient grace, Anthony Kelly is right to affirm that "in the genesis of our faith in Christ and of our knowledge of the Father, the Holy Spirit is the first in the order of our experience."[12] We experience the work of the Holy Spirit broadly and universally. However, in relation to salvation and narrowly understood, prevenient grace is the movement of the Spirit that leads us to respond to God and experience new birth. The Holy Spirit inspires (from Latin *inspirare*, "to breathe") us so that the Word becomes an event in our lives.[13] This is why prevenient grace, for Wesley, is like the porch toward the door of salvation. It reveals and awakens us to our true condition as sinful humans before God. Through it, "the possibility of repentance emerges. The need for vast change is dreadfully grasped. A hint of contrition is beginning to dawn."[14]

Prevenient grace leads to convincing grace. Wesley wrote: "The moment the Spirit of the Almighty strikes the heart of him that was till then without God in the world, it breaks the hardness of his heart, and creates all things new."[15] With our awareness of God and our sinful existence, we experience guilt and conviction. This in turn leads us to confession and repentance. What prompts people to repentance may differ from each other. What is crucial is that "by some awful providence, or by his Word applied with the demonstration of his Spirit, God touches the heart of him that lay asleep in darkness and in the shadow of death. He is terribly shaken out of his sleep."[16] Responding in faith, enabled humanity repents, receives forgiveness of sins,

9. Wesley, "Predestination Calmly Considered," in *Works* (JE) 9: 233.
10. Wesley, "Thoughts Upon Necessity," in *Works* (JE) 10: 473.
11. Collins, *The Theology of John Wesley*, 77–81.
12. Kelly, *God is Love*, 71.
13. Staples, "John Wesley's Doctrine of the Holy Spirit," 93–96.
14. Oden, *John Wesley's Scriptural Christianity*, 282.
15. Wesley, *Works* (BE) 4: 172.
16. Wesley, "The Spirit of Bondage and Adoption," in *Works* (BE) 1: 255.

Grace and Salvation

and begins a new life in Christ. These are still the work of the Holy Spirit, who is "the means by which Christ exerts His power in the believer's life and the means by which the believer is incorporated into Christ."[17]

Enabled Response in the Spirit

Whereas Roman Catholics emphasize human agency by believing that we receive grace by working for it and Calvinists emphasize divine agency by teaching that we receive grace unconditionally and irresistibly, Wesleyans offer a middle way by highlighting the Holy Spirit's enablement of human response in salvation. Salvation is both by divine agency and human action; these elements are not mutually exclusive. Although there is truth that God operates irresistibly, such actions of the Holy Spirit are related to his universal work of sustaining life and convicting people to repentance, not to personal salvation. The work of God through the Spirit among humans may be resisted at the moral and soteriological levels (Gen 6:3; Isa 63:10; Acts 7:51; John 16:8; 1 Thess 4:8; Heb 10:29).[18] It is a profound mystery of divine generosity that humans are endowed with dignity and freedom—so often misused—to accept or reject God's pleasing and perfect will for us. Wesley affirmed that God could choose, in his freedom and will, to act irresistibly in the same way he desired things to come to existence in creation. But "then man would be man no longer; his inmost nature would be changed. He would no longer be a moral agent, any more than the sun or the wind, as he would no longer be endued with liberty, a power of choosing or self-determination. Consequently he would no longer be capable of virtue or vice, or reward or punishment."[19]

God's grace is free, but it does not make humans captive to its biddings. Grace is not coercive. In fact, grace is liberating to the extent that it "makes human response possible, but grace does not determine that response."[20] "The present activity of the Holy Spirit," Adam Dodds writes, "does not ensure belief but enables it."[21] God neither bypasses human faculties nor unilaterally imposes his will upon us. In the words of second-century theologian Irenaeus, God changes our destiny "by means of persuasion, as

---

17. Hahn, "Pneumatology of Romans 8," 79.
18. Taylor, "The Relation of the Holy Spirit to the Self," 86.
19. Wesley, "The General Spread of the Gospel," in *Works* (BE) 2: 488–89.
20. Suchocki, "Wesleyan Grace," 472.
21. Dodds, "Regeneration and Resistible Grace," 40.

became a God of counsel, who does not use violent means to obtain what He desires."[22] God does not operate using *gratua invicta*, "invincible grace" that obliges humans to respond to God according to his wishes. Rather, divine grace works with *suavitas amoris*, "the gentleness of love."[23] The Spirit upholds our freedom. His work is to empower, not to overpower. In leading humans to salvation, God "did not take away your understanding, but enlightened and strengthened it. He did not destroy any of your affections; rather they were more vigorous than before. Least of all did he take away your liberty, your power of choosing good or evil; he did not force you; but being assisted by grace you, like Mary, chose the better part."[24]

What we emphasize is what Maddox calls "responsible grace." Grace demands our response and makes us accountable to our actions. This is true in conversion and throughout the Christian life. Co-operation is lifelong, which "necessarily implies the continual inspiration of God's Holy Spirit: God's breathing into the soul, and the soul's breathing back what it first receives from God; a continual action of God upon the soul, the reaction of the soul upon God."[25] Because we are enabled by grace, we cannot use our fallen and finite nature as an excuse for our rejection of God or disobedience to his will. Wesley emphasized this is his sermon from Philippians 2:12–13. Because God works in us, we have to work out our salvation with fear and trembling. This does not mean that we are co-redemptors with God, as if his work is incomplete without our co-operation. This also does not mean that God's grace is deficient, necessitating our response to complete his work in us. What is at stake, Maddox writes, is the "quality of God's character," because "the God we know in Christ is a God of love who respects our integrity and will not force his salvation upon us."[26]

Salvific grace is God's work through the Holy Spirit, who is a Person working in and with us in relationship, not automatic control. This is not a unique Wesleyan emphasis. Latin-speaking Augustine and Greek-speaking Chrysostom already underscored divine-human co-operation or synergism. Augustine underscored the necessity of divine re-enablement of fallen human will. One thing must be emphasized: the priority of enabling grace in the order of salvation. Otherwise, we might err in thinking that

22. Irenaeus, *Ad. Haer.* IV.1.1.
23. O'Callaghan, *God Ahead of Us*, 21.
24. Wesley, "The General Spread of the Gospel," in *Works* (BE) 2: 489.
25. Wesley, "The Great Privilege of Those that are Born of God," in *Works* (BE) 1: 442.
26. Maddox, *Responsible Grace*, 148.

grace enables us to enact what we have already decided to do beforehand, as if grace is the serum that only serves to boost our prior will to act.

Witness of the Spirit

Upon conversion, we receive the Holy Spirit as the seal of our redemption (Eph 4:30). This is why Paul admonishes us not to grieve him; instead, we must live in the Spirit. Reception of the Holy Spirit is one of the biblical evidences of having been saved and is the most basic meaning of what it means to be spiritual (1 Cor 12:3, 13). This has moral implications that will be discussed in the next section. For now, we will focus on the psychological significance of the Spirit's faithful presence in our lives.

The Holy Spirit works in and with us until our glorification. The evening before his death, Jesus promised his disciples that they would not be left alone like orphans (John 14:18). Jesus was concerned that they would be too demoralized by his looming absence and would forget his teachings and their mission. So he told them: "I will ask the Father, and he will give you another *Parakletos* to help you and be with you forever" (John 14:16). The word "another" is important. The Holy Spirit is "another advocate" because the Spirit will accompany the disciples in the same way Jesus did. A careful look at the Gospel of John reveals the similarity of function between Jesus Christ and the Holy Spirit.

	Jesus Christ	Holy Spirit
both "come from," are "given" and are "sent" from the Father into the world	John 3:16, 17; 5:43; 16:27, 28; 18:37	John 14:26; 15:26; 16:7, 8, 13
both are called "Holy"	John 6:69	John 14:26
both are called "Truth"	John 14:6	John 14:17; 15:26; 16:13
both are Teachers	John 13:13–14	John 14:26
both bear witness to and reveal God	John 4:25–26; 1:18; 3:34–36	John 15:26–27; 16:13–14
both are rejected by the world	John 1:11	John 14:17; 15:18–26

The Greek *allos* signifies that the Holy Spirit is of the same kind with Jesus Christ. In theological terms and using Nicene-Constantinopolitan language, the Holy Spirit "of the same substance" with the Son. Jesus has acted as the Paraclete so far, but the Spirit will soon take the same role.[27] But what does *Parakletos* mean? The term is a compound word, which literally means "called alongside" (from *para* + *klesis*). In short, in the same way that Jesus is Immanuel, "God with us," the "another *Parakletos*" will also be the same (Matt 1:23). The Spirit functions as God alongside us—or beside us—or with us. God's purpose in sending the Holy Spirit is for us not to be alone. Like Jesus, the disciples will be persecuted (John 15:20–21) so it is important that they are accompanied by divine presence. The Father does not abandon his children facing the challenges of the present and the uncertainties of the future (John 14:18).

But because of the Spirit's universal prevenient work, isn't he always with humanity? What is the difference between his presence before and after justification? The Spirit's presence remains the same, but the relationship between him and the redeemed human is different. The convicting work of the Spirit remains the same after conversion, preventing Christians from sinning and leading us to repentance when we fall into temptations. Before conversion, the Spirit's presence makes us feel guilt and shame because of our sins. This can lead to animosity. But after being born again, the Spirit's presence becomes a comforting presence, assuring us that we are children of God, thereby giving us love, joy, and peace. Wesley wrote:

> Every good gift is from God, and is given to man by the Holy Ghost . . . Have we love? It is "shed abroad in our hearts by the Holy Ghost which is given unto us." He inspires, breathes, infuses into our soul, what of ourselves we could not have. Does our spirit rejoice in God our Savior? It is "joy in the Holy Ghost." Have we true inward peace? It is "the peace of God" wrought in us by the same Spirit. Faith, peace, joy, love, are all his fruits . . . We have an inward experience of them, which we cannot find any fitter word to express.[28]

Inward feeling is important, although caution should be exercised lest we misinterpret our own experience. What is crucial is that we have the witness of the Spirit to our own spirits that we are indeed children of God (Rom 8:15–16). Quite exaggeratedly, Wesley referred to this "direct

---

27. For longer elaboration, see Turner, *The Holy Spirit and Spiritual Gifts*, 76–89.
28. Wesley, "A Farther Appeal to Men of Reason and Religion," in *Works* (BE) 11: 171.

witness" of the Spirit as "the main doctrine of the Methodists" and "the very foundation of Christianity."[29] Influenced by the Moravians, coupled with his personal search for assurance and his Aldersgate experience, Wesley emphasized the necessity of being certain that we are indeed saved. "The testimony of the Spirit," he preached, "is an inward impression on the soul, whereby the Spirit of God directly witnesses to my Spirit, that I am a child of God; that Jesus Christ hath loved me, and given Himself for me; and that all my sins are blotted out, and I, even I, am reconciled to God."[30]

Fruit of the Holy Spirit

In addition to the direct witness of the Spirit, Wesleyan theology underscores, perhaps with greater vigor, the indirect witness of the Spirit. This refers to the Christian's moral life in accordance with the qualities and virtues set forth in Scriptures. The more important witness that one is truly a child of God is not merely the presence of the Spirit, but actual living in the Spirit. The testimony of a changed life is the ultimate test of claims of new birth and inward religion. Moral transformation is expected in the believer's life in the Spirit (1 Cor 6:9–11). Having been born of the Spirit (John 3:5) and having received the Spirit (1 Cor 12:13), we are asked to live according to the Spirit (Rom 8:4).

What this means is simply to live in love, the fruit of the Spirit (Gal 5:22). It is to possess virtues in line with the character of God (Gal 5:22–23; 2 Pet 1:5–7). Without the fruit of the Spirit, we cannot love God and others (Matt 22:37–40) or love our enemies (Matt 5:43–48). Love is the prerequisite to humility (Rom 12:3) that leads to honoring others above ourselves (Rom 12:10). Love is the key to understanding how the gifts of the Spirit must be exercised in the body of Christ (1 Cor 12–14, with the love chapter in between). With the fruit of the Spirit, we can live in peace and fellowship (2 Cor 13:14). In the words of Kelly, "The holiness of the divine Spirit manifests itself in the great values . . . Such holiness is both healing and whole making. It leads to peace where before there was anger, conflict, and violence. It inspires patience and forgiveness where before there was resentment, vindictiveness, and isolation. Self-absorption and self-indulgence are replaced by self-sacrificing, other-regarding love."[31] Love and holiness must

---

29. Quoted in Arnett, "The Role of the Holy Spirit in Entire Sanctification," 24.
30. Wesley, "Witness of the Spirit," in *Works* (BE) 1: 287.
31. Kelly, *God is Love*, 74. Runyon writes: "Every Christian has the right to expect

go together. The tragic absence of the former is succinctly expressed by James Denney:

> A selfish, loveless heart can never succeed in this quest. A cold heart is not unblameable; it is either pharisaical or foul, or both. But love sanctifies. Often we only escape from our sins by escaping from ourselves; by a hearty, self-denying, self-forgetting interest in others . . . There is an ugly kind of faultlessness which is always raising its head anew in the Church; a holiness which knows nothing of love, but consists in a sort of spiritual isolation, in censoriousness, in holding up one's head and shaking off the dust of one's feet against brethren, in conceit, in condescension, in sanctimonious separateness from the freedom of common life, as though one were too good for the company which God has given him: all this is as common in the Church as it is plainly condemned in God's sight. It is an abomination in God's sight.[32]

In lavishing us with love, we see the enabling work of the Spirit again. Holiness is only possible because of the Spirit of holiness working in us (Rom 1:4). Wesley was wise in emphasizing love in his doctrine of sanctification. As the fruit of the Holy Spirit, love is the very foundation of the ethical life. It is the most important positive compelling force that motivates people to build and maintain good relationships. "Faith working by love," Wesley preached, "excludes both inward and outward sin."[33] Quite simply, love prevents us from committing sin, which ruins our relationship with God and others. Love embraces the other, the different, even the unlovable. In the words of Paul,

> Love is patient, love is kind. It does not envy, it does not boast, it is not proud. It does not dishonor others, it is not self-seeking, it is not easily angered, it keeps no record of wrongs. Love does not delight in evil but rejoices with the truth. It always protects, always trusts, always hopes, always perseveres (1 Cor 13:4–7).

The enabling work of the Spirit is also related to his other works in sanctification. Wesley used the term "inspiration" for the work of the Spirit

---

to sense the presence of God to his soul. This being touched by the Spirit of God, this participation, this *koinonia*, is precisely what has the power to transform, to bring new life, to renew the image of God." See *The New Creation*, 157; quoted in Cunningham, "A New Trajectory," 261.

32. Denney, *The Epistles to the Thessalonians*, 129–30.

33. Wesley, "The Great Privilege of Those that are Born of God," in *Works* (BE) 1: 441.

in believers, which refers to the "inward assistance of the Holy Ghost which helps our infirmities, enlightens our understanding, rectifies our will, comforts, purifies, and sanctifies us."[34] Through the Spirit of truth who enlightens us, our spiritual senses are opened so that we can hear God's voice more clearly and see his pleasing and perfect will (Rom 12:2). The Spirit enables us to see our current spiritual condition as humans in need of God's grace. He heightens our spiritual senses to God's work from without and within, so that our body, soul, and spirit are sanctified through and through. The Spirit is God's *provision* for the *process* of our sanctification.[35] Admittedly, transformation into Christ-likeness might be gradual. We progress not only in our walk with God but also continuously learn to present our bodies as living sacrifices, glorify God, forgive one another, add virtues to our faith, and get rid of ungodliness in us. The Holy Spirit's presence and our consequent obedience to his promptings allow us to grow towards maturity.

Finally, because love is a communal term, alongside the fact that the Spirit is the Spirit of communion, the Spirit-filled and Spirit-enabled life must be understood as a life in relationships. The work of the Spirit is not individualistic so that Spirit-filled living is a quality of a few individuals within the church. Rather, the Spirit works in the whole congregation effecting the entire body to live holy lives. Community existence is also not exclusive, because it is welcoming, incorporating, and reconciling. Holiness in love is necessarily missional. It invites and embraces the different other to join the communion of love that the church is.[36]

Gifts of the Spirit

The confusing debate between the Wesleyan emphasis on the fruit of the Spirit and the Pentecostal emphasis on the gifts of the Spirit does not need to lead us to abandon one in favor of the other. The Holy Spirit does not only empower believers to live the godly life. Being faithful to the Scriptures, especially in relation to the vocation of the people of God, we must underscore the work of the Spirit in enabling his people—whether the Israelites of old or the church today—to accomplish his purposes in the world. The outpouring of the Spirit in Acts 2 inaugurates the eschatological age, which like the Old Testament times, meant that the Spirit anoints his

---

34. Wesley, *Letters* 4: 39.
35. Story, "Pauline Thoughts about the Holy Spirit and Sanctification," 78–87.
36. Adewuya, "The Holy Spirit and Sanctification in Romans 8:1–17," 80.

Empowering Grace

people for specific tasks. God's promise to bless the whole world is accompanied by the promise of power so that we can become witnesses (Acts 1:8). It is only through the Spirit that the church can accomplish great things (John 1:50; 14:12).

Paul discusses the gifts of the Spirit in three of his letters: Romans, 1 Corinthians, and Ephesians. Interestingly, he treats the gifts in both Romans 12 and 1 Corinthians 12 alongside love. He even argues that possessing and exercising the gifts without love means and gains nothing (1 Cor 13:1–3). This is true both in church ministries or world mission, although the context of Romans and Corinthians is the former. The fruit of the Spirit and the gifts of the Spirit are inseparable. The former without the latter may lead to mysticism without vocation; the latter without the former may lead to mission without compassion. One of Paul's unmistakable concerns is to teach his audience that the gifts of the Spirit must not be used to vindicate oneself, especially as criteria to measure one's spiritual maturity. Instead, the gifts remind us that we exist for the sake of serving others. This is the emphasis of the body analogy found all three Pauline letters. We are parts of the body working together for the common good. Exercising spiritual gifts builds the body of Christ, unites us with each other, and helps us to become mature (Eph 4:11–13).

The juxtaposition of extraordinary and ordinary gifts is also misleading. Wesley unfortunately fell prey to this in his responses to his critics.[37] Consistent with his emphasis on salvation throughout his ministry, he highlighted ordinary gifts which were more enduring and needed in the everyday life of the Christian. This skewed his interest more toward the fruit of the Spirit and the various virtues that Christians must possess as we progress in maturity. He was also suspicious of miraculous gifts.[38] This does not mean, however, that Wesley and Wesleyan theology neglect the role of Christians and the church in the world. Our emphasis on discipleship, activism, and holistic mission indicates that we are concerned with our God-given vocation as much as Christian perfection. We resonate with Paul's concern about the Corinthian believers who use the gifts of the Spirit to erroneously elevate their spiritual status at the expense of putting others down. To be spiritual (*pneumatikos*) is not to display extraordinary gifts in the church; it is evidenced more by obeying the Great Commandments (Matt 22:37–40) and participating in the Great Commission (Matt

---

37. Maddox, *Responsible Grace*, 133.
38. Collins, *The Theology of John Wesley*, 128.

Grace and Salvation

28:19–20). As Jack Levison writes, "the heart of spirituality is not in gifts, but in the facility to preach Christ crucified, the capacity to receive revelations while stewarding (studying and teaching the Scripture), and the ability of live like Jesus."[39]

Conclusions

Peter explained that the prophecy of Joel 2:28–32 about the outpouring of the Spirit has been fulfilled at Pentecost (Acts 2:17–21). Several things must be pointed out. First, Peter claimed that the coming of the Holy Spirit happens "in the last days" (2:17), which means that we are in the last days since the Pentecost! We must not confuse the last days with the second coming. We are in the last days, but Jesus' second coming is not yet. Second, when we think of the last days, our minds immediately have pictures of destruction and suffering because of Matthew 23–24 and the book of Revelations. This is not wrong, because even Peter acknowledged that the last days will be characterized by "blood and fire and billows of smoke . . . the sun will be turned to darkness and the moon to blood" (Acts 2:19–20). However, we often miss the other important verses of the passage, because third, the last days are also characterized by the Spirit's outpouring.[40] This signifies the empowerment of God's people to communicate the Word of God to others (the gift of prophecy; 2:17–18). Along with the fact that the Spirit has come to "convict the world of its sin, and of God's righteousness, and of the coming judgment" (John 16:8), this means that the last days will also be a period when people will call on the name of the Lord to be saved (Acts 2:21). Indeed, in the words of Paul, because of the empowering work of the Spirit on his servants and his convicting work in the world, "now is the time of God's favor, now is the day of salvation" (2 Cor 6:2).

We must not be surprised that our world today suffers from a lot of destruction, suffering, and death. We have typhoons, flood, earthquakes, wars. However, our emphasis must be on the fact that this is the time of Pentecost-possibilities, when the Spirit is active in the world through the church, so that people will experience forgiveness from sin, freedom from bondage, and reconciliation with God. These are the days when the Spirit of adoption (Rom 8:15) is leading people to believe in the Lord Jesus Christ so that they can become children of God (John 1:12). These are the days when

39. Levison, "The Holy Spirit in 1 Corinthians," 34.
40. Dunn, *Pneumatology*, 211–15.

the Spirit of truth is convicting people about the world, about themselves, and about God (John 16:13). These are the days when the Spirit of holiness (Rom 1:4) is enabling Christians to live holy lives and be light and salt to the world, so that others may see our good deeds and glorify the Father (Matt 5:13–16). These are the days when the Spirit of power comes on faithful disciples so that we can become witnesses in our own Jerusalem, Judea, and to the ends of the earth (Acts 1:8). These are the days of lavish grace!

10

Cosmic Salvation

> "Creation waits in eager expectation for the children of God to be revealed . . . creation itself will be liberated from its bondage to decay and brought into the freedom and glory of the children of God"
>
> —ROMANS 8:19–21

Unfortunate preoccupation with human salvation—a clear sign of sinful self-centeredness—has caused a profound neglect of reflections about the place of creation in the story of God's work. But as we shall see here, being made in and recovery of the image of God are intertwined with our vocation as steward priests of creation. Our doctrine of salvation, therefore, must not only abandon an escapist approach that devalues the physical body and condemns the material world to worthlessness. It must also highlight that salvation is, first, the restoration both of human *being* and *vocation*. Salvation is not an individualistic and self-centered *for me* but a communal *through me*. Second, the saving work of Jesus Christ and the empowering agency of the Holy Spirit must be explained in such a way that the redemption of the cosmos is expressly understood as the work of the triune God. The Bible begins and ends with the whole earth in mind. It is proper, therefore, that a book on grace and salvation should devote a chapter that details the destiny of creation within God's overarching plan.

Cosmic Salvation

Universal Vision of Grace

The creation narrative in Genesis is not mere prelude to the grander story of humanity. We should note, first, that human beings did not even have a day to ourselves; we were created on the same day with creeping and crawling things. Moreover, humans are created from the ground (Gen 2:7). Second, creatures—in their diverse colors and shapes—were proclaimed "good" by God even prior to the appearance of humanity (Gen 1:4, 10, 12, 18, 21, 25). There is vibrancy and joy in the song of life even before humans joined the choir of earthly worshippers. The symphonies of creaturely praise expressed in both Psalms 104 and 148 show no sign of a human conductor. Third, divine blessing was uttered first to creatures before humans (Gen 1:22, 28).

The sobering reality about humanity's place in creation is powerfully reinforced by God's responses to Job's self-fixated questions. God challenges Job to look at his work in creation. "God demands," Denis Edwards writes, "that Job observe the physical universe in its immensity and mystery, and asks Job who he thinks he is in relation to this vast creation, and particularly in relation to the God who creates it all . . . Job is called both to cosmic humility and to share in God's delight in creatures."[1] It is true, however, that humans are special objects of divine attention. Psalm 8:5 says that humans are made "a little lower than the angels" and are awarded "glory and honor." This, however, is not a statement about a God-given superiority over all creation. Most readings of this psalm tend toward human narcissism. We must read the verses that immediately follow. They reiterate our role in creation as steward-priests to manage everything God has made (8:6–8). In short, our identity as "a little lower than angels" and our dignity as entities "crowned . . . with glory and honor" are intrinsically related to our role as God's appointed servants.[2]

The Creator's overflowing love welcomes creatures in inclusive embrace. God's deep investment in creation is quite surprising. We read about the Spirit hovering over the waters, creating beauty and order out of chaos (Gen 1:2). God personally takes action in causing things to being—either by directly speaking or shaping (Gen 1:3; 2:7). God "has compassion on all he has made" (Ps 145:9), opening his hand to "satisfy the desires of every living thing" (Ps 145:16). He sustains all things (Job 34:14; Heb 1:3),

---

1. Edwards, *Christian Understanding of Creation*, 7–8.
2. Lodahl and Maskiewicz, *Renewal in Love*, 31–32.

clothing flowers and caring for birds (Matt 6:30; 10:29–30). He loves the world so much that he creates humans in his image to serve as steward-priests whose mandate is to govern, prosper, and care for creation (Gen 1:26–29). Moreover, he fills creation with this presence. The earth is God's footstool (Isa 66:1), filling it with his glory (Ps 72:9; Jer 23:24; Isa 6:3) and unfailing love (Ps 33:5). Knowledge of the glory of the Lord is available on earth, because divine "invisible qualities—his eternal power and divine nature" are knowable through "what has been made" (Rom 1:20).

Groaning of Creation

The earth, ironically, is God's object of love and humanity's object of abuse. Humanity failed to fulfill its vocation, leading to the earth's current many problems. Instead of viewing our place in creation as steward-servants, we view ourselves as rulers and act as tyrants. By making humanity the center of creation, earth's purpose became solely for human enjoyment and continuing existence. Sin's corruption of humanity—most evident in idolatrous cosmic anthropocentrism—implicated creation and caused its progressive decay.[3] The entire cosmos is plunged to disorder (Greek *kosmos* literally means "order") because the appointed stewards have become rogue agents. The ecological order God instituted for symbiotic co-existence and mutual support of all creation is thrown out of balance because of human disobedience. Most of what we label as "acts of God" (referring to natural calamities such as floods and typhoons) may actually be human-induced.

Aside from the anthropic principle (i.e., creation revolves around humans at the center), a Gnostic view of material reality as essentially evil lingers even among Christians. Although this heresy was already rejected by the early fathers like Irenaeus of Lyons, it crept back into the church in views of salvation that teach the soul's departure from the physical world to return to God (while the body decays on earth). This escapist view, along with notions of the spiritual-material or sacred-secular divide, make Christians prejudiced against the value of creation. When we are convinced that this world is controlled by the evil one (1 John 5:19) and therefore must be judged (John 12:31), we develop a disdain of the world that leads to justified neglect of its well-being. Because we mistakenly view creation as "a willing crew member in Satan's hire,"[4] we wrongly conclude that its con-

---

3. Coloe, *Creation is Groaning*, 66.
4. Truesdale and Perry, *A Dangerous Hope*, 144.

tinuing descent to decay is its just punishment. This "spirituality of cosmic despair"[5] leaves no hope for nature. Indeed, in this line of thinking, the logical end for this evil world is judgment and destruction.[6]

Creation is groaning, Paul writes, because it has been subjected to frustration and it is in bondage to decay (Rom 8:20–22). This is not creation's own choice. When Adam sinned, the entire creation faced and suffered the consequence. This may be explained in two ways. First, it was Adam who caused creation's subjection to frustration. By our actions today we participate in Adam's sin and continue to cause creation to lament. Second, as James D. G. Dunn points out, with reference to Genesis 3:17–18, the agent of subjection is God himself.[7] This makes sense especially if we look at other Pauline passages (1 Cor 15:27–28; Phil 3:21; Eph 1:22). But why would God subject creation to frustration? Paul Santmire explains it by referring to "a kind of divinely mandated feedback loop" where

> God judges human sinfulness, in part at least, by "cursing the ground" because of sinful humans, who would therefore themselves have to confront thorns and thistles, instead of the plenty of Eden's garden, where they first had been placed by God (see Gen 2:17–19) . . . There is no cosmic fall, in other words, but in the aftermath of human sin, as Paul would think about these things, God reshapes the human experience of nature so that that experience is no longer a blessing but a curse.[8]

Both interpretations are not mutually exclusive. The "ecological feedback loop" in which "human excess disrupts nature, which, in turn, disrupts human life" and the "divinely mandated feedback loop" in which "God judges human sin by subjecting nature to futility, which, in turn, disrupts human life" both connect creation's frustration to human sin.[9] What is crucial is that creation itself suffers the consequence of sin as an unwilling victim. It would thus be unfair that its suffering is only a precursor to its ultimate

---

5. Santmire, *Beyond Nature*, 202.

6. Other misinterpretations that led to the ecological crisis are enumerated by Dolamo in "A Trinitarian Theology of Creation: An Ethical Perspective." They include the ideas of God's transcendence, world hierarchy of importance of creatures, human mandate to dominate creation, God's actions predominantly in history than in creation, that only humans are beneficiaries of God's redemption and grace, and the separation of secular from the sacred.

7. Dunn, *Romans 1–8*, 470–71.

8. Santmire, *Beyond Nature*, 207–8.

9. Santmire, *Beyond Nature*, 208.

destruction. Thankfully, in God's grace, it is subjected to frustration "*in hope* that creation itself will be liberated from its bondage to decay and brought to freedom and glory of the children of God" (Rom 8:21; italics mine).

Redemption of Creation

The entire creation being implicated in God's punishment for humanity's sin is clear in the Flood story (Gen 6:5–7). The whole earth is engulfed with water, killing everything except those in the ark. The order instituted by God in the separation of land from water (Gen 1:9–10) goes haywire. This can be interpreted "as an act of decreation that is a just and appropriate judgement; as humanity inflicts destruction upon creation through sinful rebellion and violence, so God permits human beings to experience the logical outcome of their evil."[10] But after de-creation is re-creation.

The Flood story teaches several things. First, divine punishment does not lead to annihilation of everything that is. God does not create an entirely new world from nothing to replace the old. In his divine sovereignty and power, God could start anew with an Earth 2.0, an entirely new planet with new sets of entities, but he chooses not to snuff out of existence that which he originally pronounced "good." Second, God's action towards creation involves a redemption plan. The other side of God's anger is his gracious willingness to give a corrupted world another chance. Third, creation is a recipient of a divine promise that secures its existence: "Never again will all life be destroyed by waters of a flood" (Gen 9:11). This covenant is "for all generations to come" (Gen 9:12) and encompasses the destiny of humans and all living creatures (Gen 9:12, 15, 16, 17). God promises to maintain cosmic order and creation's fruitfulness (Gen 1:28; 8:17).

The destiny of creation, thus, is not bleak destruction. God's plan for it is much grander. "The present creation will not be destroyed," N. T. Wright says, "rather the reverse. It will be *set free* from destruction, from the severe limitation imposed by *phthora*, 'decay'. It will be more truly itself when, in the end, God will be 'all in all.'"[11] The destiny of creation is similar to that of humanity. The parallels in Romans 8 are unmistakable. Creation is waiting "in eager anticipation for the children of God to be revealed" (8:19) in the same way humans "wait eagerly for our adoption to sonship" (8:23). Creation hopes to be delivered from decay (8:21) while

---

10. Lodahl and Maskiewicz, *Renewal in Love*, 63–64.
11. Wright, *History and Eschatology*, 138.

humans wait for "the redemption of our bodies" (8:23). In the interim, both creation and humanity groan (8:22-23). The material creation is co-heir with humanity (8:17) because the Spirit who gives life (8:1, 10) and brings us to adoption as children of God (8:14-16) is the same Spirit who can "give life to mortal bodies" (8:11).

Original creation will not be rendered null and void; it will be transfigured in the new creation. This world as we know it, is our home now and forever. William Wordsworth says it well:

> Not in Utopia—subterranean fields,—
> Or some secreted island, Heaven knows where!
> But in this world, which is the world
> Of all of us,—the place where, in the end
> We find our happiness, or not at all!

"This world in its present form is passing away" (1 Cor 7:31), but this does not imply annihilation. For Augustine "it is the form (*figura*) of the world that passes away, not its very nature (*natura*)."[12] Irenaeus also ends his *Against Heresies* with the same affirmation: "Neither is the substance nor the essence of the creation annihilated (for faithful and true is He who has established it), but the *fashion* of the world passes away" (*Adv. Haer.* 5.36.1). Irenaeus' insights are important because his theology is characterized by strong resistance to the disembodied theologies of his day, insistence on the goodness of creation, defense of the incarnation of Jesus Christ, and developmental vision of created reality. When applied to the end times, these themes "produce[s] an important counterweight to the flight from the world and the failure to take seriously the resurrection of the flesh which marks the Platonizing Christian eschatologies of a later period and indeed the average Christian consciousness."[13]

God's vision is that of cosmic peace, entailing the end of violence that characterizes current relationships within the created order. As discussed in chapter 6, the solution to sin and its consequence is forgiveness that results in reconciliation and sanctification, including the cosmos. God reveals consistency in his saving work from Genesis to Revelation. In the

---

12. Quoted in Blowers, *Drama of the Divine Economy*, 239-40.

13. von Balthasar, *The Glory of the Lord*, 93. Even the Roman Catholic Church distances itself from theologies that suggest the destruction of the material world. Instead, there are statements in major documents that speak of creation's redemption, such as in *Lumen Gentium*, 48a; *Gaudium et spes*, 39a; and *Catechism of the Catholic Church*, 1042-50; see O'Callaghan, *Christ Our Hope*, 116.

same way he liberates Israel from bondage and raises Jesus from the dead, he will set the whole creation free from bondage to decay. The new heaven and the new earth (Rev 21:1) is the current created cosmos, redeemed and transformed. "New creation" where "the old is gone and the new has come" (2 Cor 5:17) means transformation, not new formation. There is continuity and discontinuity. Isaiah's vision has the clearest picture of the continuing presence of earthly species but existing in radical discontinuity from their former instincts. Instead of violence, harmonious relationships will prosper. His vision is worth quoting in full:

> The wolf will live with the lamb,
> the leopard will lie down with the goat,
> the calf and the lion and the yearling together;
> and a little child will lead them.
> The cow will feed with the bear,
> their young will lie down together,
> and the lion will eat straw like the ox.
> The infant will play near the cobra's den,
> and the young child will put its hand into the viper's nest.
> They will neither harm nor destroy
> on all my holy mountain,
> for the earth will be filled with the knowledge of the Lord
> as the waters cover the sea (Isa. 11:6–9)

Wesley exuded the same optimism toward the transformation of creation. He believed that even heavenly bodies will change and will no longer bring harm. The earth will be renewed to exclude earthquakes, harmful plants, and malevolent creatures.[14] Earthly elements and creatures will become benign, and all creatures will become capable of knowing, loving, and enjoying God.[15] Because of this, we might expect, "the sound of weeping and of crying will be

---

14. Wesley, "The New Birth," in *Works* (BE) 2: 503, 509.

15. Wesley, "The General Deliverance," in *Works* (BE) 2: 448. Irenaeus' vision compliments Isaiah's and Wesley's: "The creation, having been renovated and set free, shall fructify with an abundance of all kinds of food, from the dew of heaven, and from the fertility of the earth . . . In like manner [the Lord declared] that a grain of wheat would produce ten thousand ears, and that every ear should have ten thousand grains, and every grain would yield ten pounds of clear, pure, fine flour; and that all other fruit-bearing trees, and seeds and grass, would produce in similar proportions; and that all animals feeding [only] on the productions of the earth, should [in those days] become peaceful and harmonious among each other, and be in perfect subjection to man" (*Adv. Haer.* 5.33.3).

heard in it no more" (Isa 65:19). The transformation is so profound, that "the former things shall not be remembered or come to mind" (Isa 65:17).

Creation Gathered in Christ

The prophet Isaiah directly relates his vision of the new creation to the person and work of the Anointed One, the Messiah upon whom the Spirit of the Lord rests (Isa 11:1–2). It is no wonder, therefore, that the New Testament adamantly locates the destiny of all creation in Jesus Christ. Several observations must be made especially from the Christological hymn of Colossians 1:15–23. First, all creation exists in, by, and for Christ: "in him all things were created . . . all things have been created through him and for him . . . [and] in him all things hold together" (Col 1:17). Everything that exists is sustained and held together in Christ (Heb 1:3). Nothing is less important. Nothing is excluded.

Second, the new creation enjoys peace because of Jesus' blood shed on the cross (Col 1:20). Enmity and alienation affected the entire earth, but Christ reconciled us to God through his death (Col 1:22). "Through his death and resurrection," John Zizioulas writes, "Christ aimed precisely at this unity and communion of the whole creation with God."[16] Revolution in world history really began the day Jesus was crucified—a revolution that established the kingdom on earth, whose subjects include all creation. Through the cross, Jesus "disarmed the powers and authorities" that create violence in the world (Col 2:15; 1 Cor 15:24). While Colossians speaks of all things reconciled in Christ, Ephesians talks of all things gathered under Christ (Eph 1:10, 22). This is where Irenaeus grounds his doctrine of recapitulation. In the same way that we all shared in Adam's sin and death, we now share in Christ's righteousness and life. Everything is now summed up in Christ. Our identity as humans and the destiny of creation are no longer bound to Adam because Jesus Christ has undone Adam's disobedience and its consequences.

Third, "he has reconciled you by Christ's physical body" (Col 1:22). The incarnation of the Son must be understood as God's initiative to restore and renew all of creation. Jesus is able to sum up creation in himself precisely because he shared in its constitution. Jesus assumed not only humanity in his incarnation; he assumed creatureliness, giving dignity to materiality and affirming its primordial goodness. "The incarnation hallows

16. Chryssavgis et al., *Toward an Ecology of Transformation*, 168.

all of creation."[17] The incarnation is the clearest biblical expression that God takes creation—its finitude, contingency, beauty, and corrupted ugliness—seriously. "Deep incarnation as enacted in Jesus' ministry," Elizabeth Johnson argues, "underscores the dignity of all that is physical, for bodies matter to God: all bodies, not only those that are beautiful and full of life but also those damaged, violated, starving, dying, bodies of humankind and otherkind alike."[18] God values creation and intervenes on its behalf, because like humans, creation cannot save itself. Since the material world is made by, in, and for Christ, its ultimate perfection is also found in his saving work.

Finally, Jesus' resurrection reveals the destiny of all material reality. Jesus' bodily resurrection "validates the permanence of the incarnation, which in turn reinforces the goodness of the material creation."[19] It serves as "the great sign of God's end for the world: life out of death, hope from ashes, light shining out of darkness."[20] If indeed the last enemy is death (2 Cor 15:26), then Jesus' victory over death has won hope of life for all creation. The Christian hope is resurrection of the body (1 Cor 15) and liberation from decay (Rom 8:21). The redemption of creation may be likened to Jesus' emergence from the tomb in glorious light. Creation will burst out to life after being confined in the darkness of decay.

The Spirit of Life in Creation

Life-giving is the role of the Holy Spirit in creation. We see the Spirit hovering over chaotic and formless earth to bring order and beauty (Gen 1:2). God's *ruach* turned a lump of clay into a living soul (Gen 2:7). An entire valley of dry bones can return to life through the Spirit's agency (Ezek 37:1–14). We should not be surprised, then, that even Jesus' resurrection is through the Spirit (1 Pet 3:18). The profound implication for our salvation is this: "If the Spirit of him who raised Jesus from the dead is living in you, he who raised Christ from the dead will also give life to your mortal bodies" (Rom 8:11).

Romans 8 extends this magnanimous gift of life to all creation. Paul begins the chapter by saying that because of Jesus' atoning work, "the law of

---

17. Lodahl and Maskiewicz, *Renewal in Love*, 79.
18. Johnson, "Jesus and the Cosmos: Soundings in Deep Christology," 145.
19. Lodahl and Maskiewicz, *Renewal in Love*, 97.
20. Lodahl and Maskiewicz, *Renewal in Love*, 129.

the Spirit who gives life" sets humans free "from the law of sin and death" (Rom 8:2). The Spirit of life liberates us from anti-life forces, particularly sin (which is the cause of death) and death (which is the consequence of sin). This applies to creation as well. Humans are set free from "mortal bodies" that are subject to death (8:11, 23) and creation is "liberated from its bondage to decay" (8:21). The language of inheritance in 8:15–17 is also important, because it is related to the work of the Spirit of adoption and the privileges of the children of God. Creation is waiting for the children of God to be revealed so that they might become "heirs of God and joint heirs with Christ" (Rom 8:17). Jesus is indeed the firstborn from the dead, whose resurrection through the Spirit is the pattern for everyone and everything else's.

Again, what is crucial here is the affirmation of physicality. When we juxtapose the Spirit with materiality, as if they are irreconcilable opposites, we miss the fact that the Spirit in the Bible is presented precisely as one "who descends on bodies in creation."[21] The Spirit cannot be seen as intrinsically antithesis to the bodily, tangible, or corporeal. The Spirit sustains creaturely life and prevents it from lapsing back into nothingness (Ps 104:10–14, 30). Merely to be alive is to be endowed with life by the Spirit. Consequently, the withdrawal of the Spirit could mean death (Job 33:4). "If it were [God's] intention and he withdrew his *ruach* (spirit) and *neshamah* (breath), all mankind would perish together and man would return to the dust" (Job 34:14–15; also Ps 104:29). This is why Eugene F. Rogers, Jr. names the Spirit as one who rests on bodies *paraphysically*.[22] The Spirit rests *para*, "alongside" the physical. In the same way that Jesus was dependent on the Spirit's empowering presence,[23] creation depends on the Spirit's life-giving work. The good news is that the Spirit is thoroughly immersed in the whole creation (Ps 139:7). With the Spirit, "the face of the ground" is "renewed" (Ps 104:30). Jensen is right: "The struggle for the life of bodies—the fecundity of the planet, the body politic, the health of infants and elderly . . . are dimensions of Spirit's movement."[24]

---

21. Jensen, *The Lord and Giver of Life*, 1.

22. Jensed, *The Lord and Giver of Life*, 87–95.

23. There is no moment in the life of Jesus when the Spirit was not operative in his life. Jesus was conceived of the Spirit (Matt 1:20; Luke 1:35), baptized with the Holy Spirit (Matt 3:16; Mark 1:10), and led by the Spirit (Matt 4:1; Mark 1:12; Luke 4:1). He was anointed by the Spirit to minister (Luke 4:16–21; fulfilling Isa 61:1–2), including driving out evil spirits (Matt 12:28). And finally, Jesus is resurrected in the power of the Holy Spirit (1 Pet 3:18).

24. Jensen, *The Lord and Giver of Life*, 2.

Grace and Salvation

The saving work of Jesus Christ and the enlivening work of the Holy Spirit reveal God's gracious engagement of and in the world and provide us hints about the already-not-yet of the kingdom. With the coming of the Messiah, the new age has dawned, the revolution has begun, and the kingdom has been inaugurated. The Holy Spirit is sent as a "down payment" (2 Cor 5:5; Eph 1:14), indicating that full redemption is yet to come (Rom 8:23). The Spirit is the link of continuity between the old creation and the new creation. It may even be said that the Spirit continues to hover over the waters of creation, acting non-stop not only to sustain its existence amidst the chaos brought by evil, but also to bring creation to its perfection. In this way, *ruach* is "a subtle but hopeful promise of life and creativity to come . . . the divine *ruach* consistently bespeaks hope in the midst of hopelessness, life in the face of death, new possibilities where none would be imagined . . . the *ruach* is brooding over new possibilities even in the face of the chaotic darkness of the deep."[25]

The Interim: Priests of Creation

The direct work of the Holy Spirit in creation, however, must be balanced with his indirect work through the people of God. This is God's consistent approach in the Scriptures. He chooses men and women, empowers them through the Holy Spirit, and guides them to accomplish his gracious work. God calls one for the sake of the many. He does not act in coercive fiat but deals with creation by calling willing mediators. We humans fill this role. The image of God, if interpreted in the light of the context of Genesis 1, is not primarily about divine qualities found in humanity. Rather, it is a calling or function to be God's representatives on earth. We are God's steward-priests whose responsibility is to manage, care, and prosper creation.[26]

Our mandate, in the words of Wesley, is to become "channel of conveyance" between God and creation.[27] But because of sin, this vocation is corrupted. We have become tyrants instead of protectors, abusers instead of managers. But God in Jesus Christ restores us in his image. This entails both reconciliation with God and recovery of our vocation as priests of creation. The renewal of humanity, therefore, is an important phase in

---

25. Lodahl and Maskiewicz, *Renewal in Love*, 23.

26. Lodahl and Maskiewicz, *Renewal in Love*, 32, 41, 102. See also Walton, *The Lost World of Adam and Eve*, 41–42.

27. Wesley, "The Great Deliverance," in *Works* (BE) 2: 440.

the redemption of the cosmos. The redemption of humanity and the establishment of the church may be likened to the calling of Abraham and the establishment of the covenant with Israel. God intends to bless all of creation through "a chosen people, a royal priesthood, a holy nation, God's special possession" (1 Pet 2:9). As we embody holiness, the redemption of the cosmos begins. New creation is a process "growing slowly and with some retrograde movements along the way, not so much in the external, politicized order but within the church."[28] Christians overflowing with the fruit of the Spirit in their lives serve their human and non-human neighbor.

The vision of the new heaven and new earth, therefore, must not breed passivity. Divine intervention does not abolish human agency; it requires it. God's grace makes us responsible citizens of the kingdom. We are redeemed to participate in God's mission. "Expecting God's eschatological reign to come means both to trust and to be on mission: to trust in the coming of God's eschatological reign and to actively engage in liberating earthly realities from all sorts of oppression—one not without the other."[29] This means two things. First, the Christian agenda is to live out in the present what is anticipated in the future. If the biblical future we imagine is characterized by peaceful cohabitation and vibrant creation, then we strive, in the enabling power of the Spirit, to embody such future in our daily lives now. This is God's grace at work *in* us. Second, our Christian mission includes energetic proclamation against creation abuse and injustice, engagement in creation protection and conservation, and active participation in all pro-earth initiatives. This is God's grace at work *through* us.

In the interim, between now and the future, the already and the not-yet, our task is primarily to love. This is what it means to be Wesleyan in truth and in deed. But this love should be inclusive of all creation and must encompass both the present and the future. The questions we should ask are these: "How do we live in the present moment in such a way as to love *our neighbor of the future* as we love ourselves? How shall we live now such that our lives are an expression of divine love for those creatures yet to come, human and nonhuman? Does not God love them as well?"[30]

---

28. Collins, "The New Creation as a Multivalent Theme in John Wesley's Theology," 96.

29. Urbaniak and Otu, "How to Expect God's Reign to Come;" Himes, "Israel and Her Vocation."

30. Lodahl and Maskiewicz, *Renewal in Love*, 48.

Bibliography

Ackerman, David. "The High Priesthood of Jesus and the Sanctification of Believers in Hebrews 7–10." *Wesleyan Theological Journal* 45 (2010) 226–45.

Ackyord, Peter R. *Exile and Restoration: A Study of Hebrew Thought of the Sixth Century BC.* Philadelphia: Westminster, 1968.

Adewuya, J. Ayodeji. "The Holy Spirit and Sanctification in Romans 8:1–17." *Journal of Pentecostal Theology* 9 (2001) 71–84.

Albertz, Rainer. *A History of Israelite Religion in the Old Testament Period.* Vol. 2, *From the Exile to the Maccabees.* Louisville, KY: Westminster John Knox, 1994.

———. *Israel in Exile: The History and Literature of the Sixth Century B.C.E.* Translated by David Green. Atlanta: SBL, 2003.

Arnett, William M. "The Role of the Holy Spirit in Entire Sanctification in the Writings of John Wesley." *Wesleyan Theological Journal* 14 (1979) 15–29.

Aulén, Gustaf. *Christus Victor: An Historical Study of the Three Main Types of the Idea of Atonement.* New York: Macmillan, 1958.

Baab, Otto J. "The God of Redeeming Grace: Atonement in the Old Testament." *Interpretation* 10 (1956) 131–43.

Banks, R., ed. *Reconciliation and Hope: New Testament Essays on Atonement and Eschatology.* Grand Rapids: Eerdmans, 1974.

Barrick, William D. "The Mosaic Covenant." *The Master's Seminary Journal* 10 (1999) 213–32.

Barth, Karl. *Dogmatics in Outline.* New York: Harper & Row, 1959.

Bauckham, Richard. *Bible and Mission.* Grand Rapids: Baker Academic, 2004.

Beeke, Joel R. "Our Glorious Adoption: Trinitarian Based and Transformed Relationships." *Puritan Reformed Journal* 3 (2011) 63–79.

Blowers, Paul. *Drama of the Divine Economy: Creator and Creation in Early Christian Theology and Piety.* Oxford: Oxford University Press, 2012.

Boff, Leonardo. *Holy Trinity: Perfect Community.* Translated by Phillip Berryman. Maryknoll, NY: Orbis, 2000.

Bibliography

Bonhoeffer, Dietrich. *Creation and Fall, Temptation: Two Biblical Studies.* New York: MacMillan, 1959.

Borg, Marcus J., and N. T. Wright. *The Meaning of Jesus: Two Visions.* New York: HarperCollins, 1999.

Bryan, Steven M. "The End of Exile: The Reception of Jeremiah's Prediction of a Seventy-Year Exile." *Journal of Biblical Literature* 137 (2018) 107–26.

Brueggemann, Walter. *Genesis.* Atlanta: John Knox, 1982.

———. *Hopeful Imagination: Prophetic Voice in Exile.* Philadelphia: Fortress, 1986.

———. *Reverberations of Faith: A Theological Handbook of Old Testament Themes.* Louisville: Westminster John Knox, 2002.

———. *Theology of the Old Testament: Testimony, Dispute, Advocacy.* Minneapolis: Fortress, 1997.

Burroughs, Presian. "Wesley's Presentation of Salvation in 'The Scripture Way of Salvation': A Pauline Assessment." *Wesleyan Theological Journal* 51 (2016) 203–8.

Campbell, George Van Pelt. "Refusing God's Blessing: An Exposition of Genesis 11:27–32." *Bibliotheca Sacra* 165 (2008) 268–82.

Carson, D. A. "Reflections on Salvation and Justification in the New Testament." *Journal of Evangelical Theological Society* 40 (1997) 581–608.

Cell, George Croft. *The Rediscovery of John Wesley.* Lanham: University Press of America, 1983.

Cherry, Natalya. "Wesley's Doctrinal Distinctions in Developing the Faith that Marks the New Birth." *Wesleyan Theological Journal* 52 (2017) 100–112.

Clemens, David M. "The Law of Sin and Death: Ecclesiastes and Genesis 1–3." *Themelios* 19 (1994) 5–8.

Clines, David J. A. *The Theme of the Pentateuch.* Sheffield: Journal for the Study of the Old Testament, 1982.

Coleson, Joseph E. *"Ezer Cenegdo": A Power Like Him, Facing Him as Equal.* Indianapolis: Wesleyan/Holiness Women Clergy, 1996.

Collins, C. John. "What Happened to Adam and Eve?" A Literary-Theological Approach to Genesis 3." *Presbyterion* 27 (2011) 12–44.

Collins, Kenneth J. "The New Creation as a Multivalent Theme in John Wesley's Theology." *Wesleyan Theological Journal* 37 (2002) 77–102.

———. *The Theology of John Wesley: Holy Love and the Shape of Grace.* Nashville: Abingdon, 2007.

Collins, Kenneth J., and Christine Johnson. "From the Garden to the Gallows: The Significance of Free Grace in the Theology of John Wesley." *Wesleyan Theological Journal* 48 (2013) 7–29.

Coloe, Mary L. *Creation is Groaning: Biblical and Theological Perspectives.* Collegeville, MN: Liturgical, 2013.

Coulson, John R. "Jesus and the Spirit in Paul's Theology: The Earthly Jesus." *Catholic Biblical Quarterly* 79 (2017) 77–96.

Cranfield, C. E. B. *A Critical and Exegetical Commentary on the Epistle to the Romans.* Edinburgh: T. & T. Clark, 1979.

Crawford, Nathan. "Pursuing an Ontology of Attunement through St. Augustine's Christology." *Wesleyan Theological Journal* 45 (2010) 179–96.

Chryssavgis, et al., eds. *Toward an Ecology of Transformation.* New York: Fordham University Press, 2013.

Cunningham, Joseph W. "A New Trajectory in Wesleyan Pneumatology: 'Perceptible Inspiration" Reconsidered." *Wesleyan Theological Journal* 45 (2010) 242–61.

Bibliography

Davies, John A. *A Royal Priesthood: Literary and Intertextual Perspectives on an Image of Israel in Exodus 19:6*. London: T. & T. Clark, 2004.

Davis, John P. "Who are the Heirs of the Abrahamic Covenant?" *Evangelical Review of Theology* 29 (2005) 149–63.

Denney, James. *The Epistles to the Thessalonians*. New York: A. C. Armstrong, 1892.

Deschner, John. *Wesley's Christology: An Interpretation*. Dallas: Southern Methodist University Press, 1985.

Dodds, Adam. "Regeneration and Resistible Grace: A Synergistic Proposal." *Evangelical Quarterly* 83 (2011) 29–48.

Dolamo, Ramathate T. H. "A Trinitarian Theology of Creation: An Ethical Perspective." *HTS Teologiese Studies/Theological Studies* 75.1 (2019) 1–8. https://doi.10.4102/hts.v75i1.5421.

Dunn, James D. G. *The Christ and the Holy Spirit*, vol. 2, *Pneumatology*. Grand Rapids: Eerdmans, 1998.

———. *Romans 1–8*. Word Biblical Commentary. Dallas: Word, 1988.

Edgar, Brian. *The Message of the Trinity: Life in God*. Leicester: IVP, 2004.

Edwards, Denis. *Christian Understanding of Creation*. Philadelphia: Augsburg Fortress, 2017.

Emmrich, Martin. "The Temptation Narrative of Genesis 3:1–6: Prelude to the Pentateuch and the History of Israel." *Evangelical Quarterly* 73 (2001) 3–20.

Eugenio, Dick O. "Following Jesus the Reconciler." In *Following Jesus: Prophet, Priest, King*, edited by Timothy R. Gaines and Kara Lyons-Pardue, 95–108. Kansas City: Foundry, 2018.

Fretheim, Terence E. *The Pentateuch*. Nashville: Abingdon, 2003.

Gathercole, S. J. *Where Is Boasting? Early Jewish Soteriology and Paul's Response in Romans 1–5*. Grand Rapids: Eerdmans, 2002.

Greathouse, William M. *Wholeness in Christ: Toward a Biblical Theology of Holiness*. Kansas City: Beacon Hill, 1998.

Gordon, Robert P. "Barak." In *New International Dictionary of the Old Testament and Exegesis*, edited by Willem VanGemeren, 757–68. Grand Rapids: Zondervan, 1996.

Gschwandtner, Christina M. "Sharing Our Weakness: Christ, Creation, and Fallenness." *Wesleyan Theological Journal* 45 (2010) 164–78.

Gunter, W. Stephen. *The Limits of Love Divine*. Nashville: Kingswood, 1989.

Hagner, Donald A. *Matthew 1–13*. Dallas: Word, 1993.

Hahn, Roger L. "Pneumatology in Romans 8: It's Historical and Theological Context." *Wesleyan Theological Journal* 21 (1986) 74–90.

Hambrick, Matthew, and Michael Lodahl. "Responsible Grace in Christology? John Wesley's Rendering of Jesus in the Epistle to the Hebrews." *Wesleyan Theological Journal* 43 (2008) 86–103.

Hamilton, Victor P. *The Book of Genesis Chapters 1–17*. Grand Rapids: Eerdmans, 1990.

Heineqq, Peter. "The Ecological Curse: A Reading of Genesis 3." *Cross Currents* (2015) 441–47.

Himes, Paul A. "Israel and Her Vocation: The Fourth Stage of Romans 11." *Bibliotheca Sacra* 176 (2019) 35–50.

Holmes, Stephen. *The Wondrous Cross: Atonement and Penal Substitution in the Bible and History*. Milton Keynes: Paternoster, 2007.

Jensen, David, ed. *The Lord and Giver of Life: Perspectives on Constructive Pneumatology*. London: Westminster John Knox, 2008.

Bibliography

Jipp, Jonathan W. "Rereading the Story of Abraham, Isaac, and 'Us' in Romans 4." *Journal for the Study of the New Testament* 32 (2009) 217–42.

Johnson, Elizabeth A. "Jesus and the Cosmos: Soundings in Deep Christology." In *Incarnation: On the Scope and Depth of Christology*, edited by N. H. Gregersen, 133–56. Minneapolis: Fortress, 2015.

Johnson, Luke Timothy. "Hebrews' Challenge to Christians: Christology and Discipleship." In *Preaching Hebrews*, edited by David Fleer and Dave Bland, 11–28. Abilene, TX: Abilene Christian University Press, 2003,

Kaiser, Walter C., Jr. *A History of Israel*. Nashville, TN: Broadman and Homan, 1998.

———. *Mission in the Old Testament: Israel as a Light to the Nations*. Grand Rapids: Baker, 2000.

Keener, Craig S. *A Commentary on the Gospel of Matthew*. Grand Rapids: Eerdmans, 1999.

Kelly, Anthony J. *God is Love*. Collegeville, MN: Liturgical, 2012.

King, Yvette. "The Progressive Announcement of Salvation in Luke, Revealing a Shift in Redemptive History." *Journal of Biblical Theology* 2 (2019) 5–28.

Lee, Chee-Chiew. "Once Again: The Niphal and the Hithpael of בָּרַךְ in the Abrahamic Blessing for the Nations." *Journal for the Study of the New Testament* 36 (2012) 279–96.

———. "בָּרַךְ in Genesis 35:11 and the Abrahamic Promise of Blessings for the Nations." *Journal of the Evangelical Theological Society* 52 (2009) 467–82.

Lee, Mason. "'Now Is the Acceptable Time, Now Is the Day of Salvation': Reading 2 Corinthians 5:11—6:2 in Light of its Narrative Substructure." *Restoration Quarterly* 56 (2014) 1–13.

Letham, Robert. "'Not a Covenant of Works in Disguise' (Herman Bavinck): The Place of the Mosaic Covenant in Redemptive History." *Mid-America Journal of Theology* (2013) 143–77.

Levison, Jack. "The Holy Spirit in 1 Corinthians." *Interpretation* 72 (2018) 29–42.

Lightenstein, Murray H. "The Fearsome Sword of Genesis 3:24." *Journal of Biblical Literature* 134 (2015) 53–57.

Lodahl, Michael. *God of Nature and of Grace: Reading the World in a Wesleyan Way*. Nashville: Kingswood, 2003.

———. *The Story of God*. 2nd ed. Kansas City: Beacon Hill, 2008.

Lodahl, Michael, and April Cordero Maskiewicz. *Renewal in Love: Living Holy Lives in God's Good Creation*. Kansas City: Beacon Hill, 2014.

Maddox, Randy. *Responsible Grace: John Wesley's Practical Theology*. Nashville: Kingswood, 1994.

Massey, James Earl. "Reconciliation: The Biblical Imperative and Practical Implications." *Wesleyan Theological Journal* 37 (2002) 7–24.

McFarland, Orrey. "Whose Abraham, Which Promise? Genesis 5:16 in Philo's *De Virtutibus* and Romans 4." *Journal for the Study of the New Testament* 34 (2012) 107–29.

Moltmann, Jürgen. *The Church in the Power of the Spirit*. New York: Harper and Row, 1977.

———. "Perichoresis: An Old Magic Word for a New Trinitarian Theology." In *Trinity, Community and Power: Mapping Trajectories in Wesleyan Theology*, edited by M. Douglas Meeks, 111–25. Nashville: Kingswood, 2000.

Mozley, J. K. *The Doctrine of Atonement*. London: Gerald Duckworth, 1953.

Muilenburg, James. "Abraham and the Nations: Blessing and World History." *Interpretation* 9 (1965) 387–98.

Bibliography

Muis, Jan. "Justification and the Justice of God: Barth's View." *Zeitschrift für Dialektische Theologie*, Supplement Series 6 (2014): 177–94.
Nelson, Richard D. "'He Offered Himself': Sacrifice in Hebrews." *Interpretations* 57 (2003) 251–65.
Neyrey, Jerome H. *Imagining Jesus in His Own Culture: Creating Scenarios of the Gospel for Contemporary Prayer.* Eugene, OR: Cascade, 2018.
Noble, Tom. *Holy Trinity, Holy People: The Theology of Christian Perfecting.* Eugene, OR: Wipf & Stock, 2013.
O'Callaghan, Paul. *Christ Our Hope: An Introduction to Eschatology.* Washington, DC: The Catholic University of America Press, 2012.
———. *God Ahead of Us.* Minneapolis, MN: Augsburg Fortress, 2014.
Oden, Thomas C. *John Wesley's Scriptural Christianity: A Plain Exposition of His Teaching on Christian Doctrine.* Grand Rapids: Zondervan, 1994.
Parker, Julie Faith. "Blaming Eve Alone: Translation, Omission, and Implications of עִמָּהּ in Genesis 3:6b." *Journal of Biblical Literature* 132 (2013) 729–47.
Parvan, Alexandra. "Genesis 1–3: Augustine and Origen on the Coats of Skins." *Vigiliae Christianae* 66 (2012) 59–92.
Plato. *Five Works of Plato.* Edited by A. D. Lindsay. London: J. M. Dent and Sons, 1927.
Porter, Calvin L. "The Salvation Story in the New Testament." *Encounter* 35 (1974) 153–62.
Pyne, Robert A. "The 'Seed,' the Spirit, and the Blessings of Abraham." *Bibliotheca Sarca* 152 (1995) 211–22.
Rendtorff, Rolf. "'Covenant' as a Structuring Concept in Genesis and Exodus." *Journal of Biblical Literature* 108 (1989) 385–93.
Roberts, Alexander, et al., eds. *Ante Nicene Fathers.* Vol. 1, *Apostolic Fathers.* Grand Rapids: Eerdmans, 1950.
Rotenberry, Paul. "Blessing in the Old Testament: A Study of Genesis 12:3." *Restoration Quarterly* 2 (1958) 32–36.
Runyon, Theodore. *The New Creation: John Wesley's Theology Today.* Nashville: Abingdon, 1998.
———. "The New Creation: The Wesleyan Distinctive." *Wesleyan Theological Journal* 31 (1996) 5–19.
Rylaarsdam, J. Coert. "Jewish-Christian Relationships: The Two Covenants and the Dilemmas of Christology." In *Grace Upon Grace: Essays in Honor of Lester J. Kuyper,* edited by James I. Cook, 70–84. Grand Rapids: Eerdmans, 1975.
Santmire, H. Paul. *Beyond Nature: A Christian Spirituality.* Philadelphia: Augsburg Fortress, 2014.
Schaff, Philip, and Henry Wace, eds. *Nicene and Post-Nicene Fathers of the Christian Church.* Second Series. Reprint. Grand Rapids: Eerdmans, 1980.
Simonetti, Manlio, ed. *Ancient Christian Commentary on Scripture: Matthew 1–13.* Downers Grove, IL: InterVarsity, 2001.
Smith-Christopher, Daniel L. *A Biblical Theology of Exile.* Minneapolis: Fortress, 2002.
Soller, Moshe. "A Latch and Clasp Connecting Deuteronomy 33:27–29 with Genesis 3:22–24: A Proposed Interpretation." *Jewish Bible Quarterly* 34 (2006) 12–15.
Staples, Rob. "John Wesley's Doctrine of the Holy Spirit." *Wesleyan Theological Journal* 21 (1986) 91–115.
Story, J. Lyle. "Pauline Thoughts about the Holy Spirit and Sanctification: Provision, Process, and Consummation." *Journal of Pentecostal Theology* 18 (2009) 67–94.

Bibliography

Suchocki, Marjorie. "Wesleyan Grace." In *The Oxford Handbook of Methodist Studies*, edited by William J. Abraham and James E. Kirby, 559–72. Oxford: Oxford University Press, 2009.

Taylor, Richard. "The Relation of the Holy Spirit to the Self." *Wesleyan Theological Journal* 22 (1987) 84–91.

Torrance, Alan. *Persons in Communion: Trinitarian Descriptions and Human Participation*. Edinburgh: T. & T. Clark, 1996.

Torrance, Thomas F. *Atonement: The Person and Work of Christ*. Edited by Robert T. Walker. Downers Grove, IL: IVP Academic, 2009.

———. *Karl Barth: Biblical and Evangelical Theologian*. Edinburgh: T. & T. Clark, 1990.

———. *The Mediation of Christ*. New ed. Edinburgh: T. & T. Clark, 1992.

———. "Proselyte Baptism." *New Testament Studies* 1 (1954) 150–54.

———. *Trinitarian Perspectives: Toward Doctrinal Agreement*. Edinburgh: T. & T. Clark, 1994.

Townsend, Jeffrey L. "Fulfillment of the Land Promise in the Old Testament." *Bibliotheca Sacra* 142 (1985) 320–37.

Truesdale, Al, and Bonnie Perry. *A Dangerous Hope: Encountering the God of Grace*. Kansas City: Beacon Hill, 1997.

Turner, Max. *The Holy Spirit and Spiritual Gifts in the New Testament Church and Today*. Revised ed. Peabody, MA: Hendrickson, 1998.

Urbaniak, J., and E. Out. "How to Expect God's Reign to Come: From Jesus' through the Ecclesial to the Cosmic Body." *HTS Teologiese Studies/Theological Studies* 72.4 (2016) a3380. http://dx.doi.org/10.4102/hts.v72i4.3380.

Vail, Eric M. *Atonement and Salvation: The Extravagance of God's Love*. Kansas City: Beacon Hill, 2016.

van der Platt, Jan G., ed. *Salvation in the NT: Perspectives on Soteriology*. Leiden: Brill, 2005.

VanGemeren, Willem. *The Progress of Redemption: The Story of Salvation from Creation to the New Jerusalem*. Grand Rapids: Zondervan, 1988.

van Houwelingen, P. H. R. "The Redemptive-Historical Dynamics of the Salvation of 'All Israel' (Rom. 11:26a)." *Calvin Theological Journal* 46 (2011) 301–14.

Vasholz, Robert. "The Character of Israel's Future in Light of the Abrahamic and Mosaic Covenants." *Trinity Journal* 25 (2004) 39–59.

von Balthasar, Hans Urs. *The Glory of the Lord: A Theological Aesthetics, II. Studies in Theological Style: Clerical Styles*. Edinburgh: T. & T. Clark, 1984.

von Rad, Gerhard. *Biblical Interpretations in Preaching*. Translated by John E. Steely. Nashville: Abingdon, 1977.

Walton, John H. *The Lost World of Adam and Eve*. Downers Grove, IL: InterVarsity, 2015.

———. *The Lost World of Genesis One: Ancient Cosmology and the Origins Debate*. Downers Grove, IL: InterVarsity Academic, 2009.

Watson, Thomas. *A Body of Practical Divinity*. London: A. Fullarton, 1845.

Walzer, Michael. *Exodus and Revolution*. New York: Basic, 1985.

Webber, Robert E. *Worship Old and New*. Rev. ed. Grand Rapids: Zondervan, 1994.

Wesley, John. *The Letters of John Wesley*, 8 vols. Edited by John Telford. London: Epworth, 1931.

———. *The Works of John Wesley*. Vol. 1, *Sermons 1–33*. Edited by Albert C. Outler. Bicentennial edition. Nashville: Abingdon, 1984.

———. *The Works of John Wesley*. Vol. 2, *Sermons 34–70*. Edited by Albert C. Outler. Bicentennial edition. Nashville: Abingdon, 1985.

Bibliography

———. *The Works of John Wesley.* Vol. 3, *Sermons 71–114.* Edited by Albert C. Outler. Bicentennial edition. Nashville: Abingdon, 1986.

———. *The Works of John Wesley.* Vol. 11, *The Appeals to Men of Reason and Religion and Certain Related Open Letters.* Edited by R. Gerald Cragg. Bicentennial edition. Nashville: Abingdon, 1987.

———. *The Works of the Rev. John Wesley,* vol. 9. Edited by Thomas Jackson. Grand Rapids: Zondervan, 1958.

———. *The Works of the Rev. John Wesley,* vol. 10. Edited by Thomas Jackson. Grand Rapids: Zondervan, 1958.

Westermann, C. *Genesis 1–11.* Translated by J. J. Scullion. Minneapolis: Fortress, 1994.

Witherington, Ben. "Salvation and Health in Christianity Antiquity: The Soteriology of Luke-Acts in its First Century Setting." In *Witness to the Gospel: The Theology of Acts,* edited by I. Howard Marshall and David Peterson, 145–66. Grand Rapids: Eerdmans, 1998.

Wong, Ka Leung. "Profanation/Sanctification and the Past, Present and Future of Israel in the Book of Ezekiel." *Journal for the Study of the Old Testament* 28 (2003) 201–39.

Wood, Darren Cushman. "Suffering with the Crucified Christ: The Function of the Cross in the Works of John Wesley and Dorothee Soelle." *Wesleyan Theological Journal* 43 (2008) 184–202.

Wright, Christopher. *Salvation Belongs to Our God: Celebrating the Bible's Central Story.* Carlisle: Langham, 2013.

Wright, N. T. *The Challenge of Jesus: Rediscovering Who Jesus Was and Is.* Downers Grove, IL: InterVarsity, 1999.

———. *The Day the Revolution Began: Reconsidering the Meaning of Jesus's Crucifixion.* San Francisco: HarperOne, 2016.

———. *History and Eschatology: Jesus and the Promise of Natural Theology.* Waco, TX: Baylor University Press, 2019.

———. *Paul and the Faithfulness of God.* Minneapolis: Fortress, 2013.

Zimmerli, Walther. *A Commentary on the Book of the Prophet Ezekiel Chapters 25–38.* Translated by James D. Martin. Philadelphia: Fortress, 1983.

www.ingramcontent.com/pod-product-compliance
Lightning Source LLC
Chambersburg PA
CBHW070916160426
43193CB00011B/1477